an alternative future for AMERICA II

an alternative future for
AMERICA II

**essays and speeches
ROBERT THEOBALD**

THE **SWALLOW PRESS** INC.

CHICAGO

Second edition
Second printing 1971

Published by
The Swallow Press Incorporated
1139 South Wabash Avenue
Chicago, Illinois 60605

This book is printed on 100% recycled paper

LIBRARY OF CONGRESS CATALOG CARD NUMBER 71-97027
ISBN 0-8040-0004-2

Grateful acknowledgment is given the following for·their per-
mission to reprint material written by Robert Theobald. Yale
Divinity School for "The Problem" (under different title),
from *Reflection,* November 1967. Bobbs-Merrill Company,
Inc. for "Women", from *Dialogue on Women.* The Los Angeles
Times for "Ecology: A Dangerous Crusade" (under different
title), from their February 8, 1970 issue. United Church of
Christ, Council for Higher Education for "Freedom in Education," from *Journal,* April 1969.

To the power you have left and
To the freedom you have coming.
May you use the former to secure the latter.

Some will say that the initiatives suggested herein are impossible. Our only reply to such a charge is that we must all therefore dare to do the impossible. All current initiatives within the realm of the possible appear to be failing.

Editors

Contents

Preface to First Edition

The United States is the most powerful nation in history, but it now appears that the price of such national power is the increasing — and eventually complete — powerlessness of the individual citizen. The almost perpetual state of civil strife which has recently emerged can be seen as a direct result of the refusal of rapidly growing numbers of people to accept this intolerable condition of powerlessness. Unfortunately, the tactics of lawlessness and violence used by those who seek to remedy their powerless condition are giving rise to an equally intolerable condition of social anarchy. The counter-tactics of repression are in turn leading us to the development of that very thing we have all thought can't happen here: the police state. Nobody will be free in America, and few will have any real power over their own lives, if it becomes necessary to have policemen and/or soldiers on every street corner of our cities. And yet such a prospect is clearly possible in the light of recent events.

Americans neither deserve nor want such a future, nor do they have to accept such a future. Traditionally, Americans have looked forward to a future of increased freedom rather than diminished freedom. Such a future still lies before us, but to get there we must change some of our social and psychological attitudes. Our present social and psychological attitudes are leading us to disaster.

We, a group of students and one faculty member, formed an experimental course last fall for the pur-

x

pose of discovering the social and psychological attitudes which are necessary to the development and maintenance of personal autonomy in a technologically routinized, bureaucratically organized society. It was clear to us that an alternative to our present future of diminished freedoms must be based upon an alternative to our present view of man as a creature to be externally coerced, shaped or otherwise conformed to pre-existing and ultimately arbitrary social norms and standards. We were making only minimal progress in the course until Robert Theobald, who spoke on our campus in September, made a number of subsequent visits to our class on his own initiative to share his concern about the growing powerlessness of the American citizen.

Many of us have accepted too small a world

Mr. Theobald's ideas made sense to us for three reasons. They articulated our own feeling of frustration with a society whose main response to the crisis of social disintegration is to enforce more rigidly the unsatisfactory socioeconomic arrangements and to escalate the paternalistic welfare-state programs which account for the uprising of the powerless in the first place. His ideas also suggested alternative arrangements and programs which were compatible with our concern for personal autonomy. Most important, they embodied the very social and psychological attitudes — the new view of man — we had been seeking.

Following one of his visits to our class, Mr. Theobald indicated his willingness to let us publish those of his articles which we found most relevant to our concern with the growing national crisis. We soon discovered, however, that some of these "articles" did not exist. Mr. Theobald had shared many ideas with us which were not in print. We therefore advised him on which ideas we wished him to elaborate in forthcoming speeches. This he did, taped them, and sent them to us for transcription ("The Prevailing Mindset," "The New Reality," and "Glimpses of an Alternative Future"). . . .

Given our primary concern with the increasing powerlessness of the individual American citizen, we have not included Mr. Theobald's thoughts on the poor countries and other aspects of international economics.[1] The materials we have chosen are organized from the general to the specific, according to three questions which were uppermost in our minds: "What are the present realities, and what type of future do they imply?" "What would an alternative, humanized future look like?" and "How do we begin to invent this alternative future?"

A book, like a sentence, customarily expresses a complete thought, only more so. This volume, consisting of a selection of thoughts on a number of related subjects, is not complete in the sense implied by the word "book." Some of the material is taken from speeches which were delivered extemporaneously, and is thus highly informal in style. Other material is quoted from a broader and more formal context which answered many of the questions that some readers will raise (we have attempted to assist such readers with bibliographical references to this larger context). The selections in this volume were originally addressed to very different audiences over a period of six years (but mostly over the last twelve months); as always happens in adopting such a format, the materials chosen give rise to some inconsistencies, repetitions, information gaps, etc., which are not ordinarily tolerated in a book.

But, to repeat, we do not consider this a book. It is a work in progress. It is a collection of associated thoughts on their way to becoming a system of thought. We found them so crucial to our present situation that we were moved to present them while still in their formative stages. For if they are not yet unified into a systematic, reasoned discourse, they are nevertheless immediately relevant. The year 1968 is a turning point in American history, and the summer of 1968 is its pivot. Thus, although this could have been a better book (in the formal sense) by next fall, the ideas need to be considered now!

It is clear to Mr. Theobald and to ourselves that if meaningful and effective initiatives are not developed immediately and extensively, we can this year reach the point of no return in the development of an oppressive police state which will ultimately reach into all facets of our lives — not because anybody wants this type of society but because repression seems to be the only response to crisis which the established authorities are readily able and willing to make. At present we see growing lawlessness and violence met only with growing forces of repression, with little being done to alleviate the causes of lawlessness and violence. We therefore see repression leading to further lawlessness and violence, which in turn leads to still further repression. At the end of this self-propelling process we see the death of all the freedoms we have been taught as Americans to hold dear.

But we also see hope in man's ability to act upon a new, positive view of human nature. The substance of this hope lies in our knowledge that there are already men who have demonstrated this ability, one of whom we know personally and now introduce to a wider audience. We deeply regret that we can introduce only his words, rather than the man himself, because ultimately it is Robert Theobald the man who catalyzed us and has catalyzed others to positive action. Had it been in our power we would have given him a network television series rather than this volume. His ideas for television programming would provide a welcome summer replacement for the self-fulfilling prophecy of pessimism and violence which characterizes present televising of the country's affairs.

Robert Theobald embodies what this country needs — a self-fulfilling prophecy of optimism and trust in the free individual. The following pages are suggestive of an alternative American future based on such a self-fulfilling prophecy. We are reasonably certain that such a future is probable in the long run, given its compatibility with fundamental American values. We would not be so concerned about this future if the existence of a long run were assured. But given the possibility that in the *short* run we all are dead (in spirit, if not in body), we join Mr. Theobald in urging the deliberate hastening of this alternative future. It is clear that such a hastening will come about only by our adoption and subsequent self-fulfillment of a more positive prophecy than the one presently prevailing. The likelihood of such an adoption on a wide scale depends upon the development of a national dialogue on alternative futures for mankind in general. This volume is intended to spark such a dialogue.

Although we realize that the following pages convey only an impression rather than a dissertation of Mr. Theobald's current thinking, we think that our selections have done justice to his ideas. We hope that the reader will do justice to them also by adding his efforts to the national dialogue on alternative futures. (for more information about this dialogue, write Mr. Robert Theobald, c/o The Center for Curriculum Design, Kendall College, Evanston, Illinois 60204.)

Only if the reader does his part will this book inspire

a rejuvenation of the dying American tradition of personal and local freedom and initiative.

Eric Baker
Richard DiDomenico
Charles Fahlstrom
Stephen Groshek
Paul Krienitz
Noel McInnis
Cynthia Pisani
Michael Salon
Jeffrey Shaw
Kathi Wilson

Kendall College
April 1968

[1] See Robert Theobald, *The Rich and The Poor: A Study of the Economics of Rising Expectations* and *The Challenge of Abundance* pp. 163-228.

Preface to Second Edition

As I review the preface to the first edition, I am particularly struck by the prophetic sentence, "The year 1968 is a turning point in American history, and the summer of 1968 is its pivot." And in the text of that edition I am similarly struck by the following passage which Robert Theobald spoke in the spring of 1968: ". . . we have something like six to nine months to make visible the beginning of a change from a society of coercive authority to a society of shared power. If conditions continue along present lines, if trends continue to develop as they are presently developing, we will move into a fascist police state in this country. . . . I am not arguing that anybody wants a fascist police state. There are few evil men around: our problem is a lack of imagination rather than a problem of evil. We are being forced toward a fascist police state by events and we will continue to be forced by events unless we change our attitudes. The fact that the development of such a police state will be unwilled does not make it less real."

Given the above statements in the spring of 1968, the events surrounding the Democratic Convention and the continued escalation of violence and repression since that time would seemingly make a second edition of this book an anachronism. Yet, copies of the first edition were steadily purchased by thousands of Americans in the United States and Canada — people who were still hopeful despite the fact that the vision of an alternative future seemed increasingly less likely of achievement. Many of these, especially young people, by letter or in person, shared their hope with us and with one another — a hope that the initiative begun by our book would continue. The growth and intensity of this shared hope convinced us to use further the power we had left in order to realize the freedom we had coming.

Therefore, in the winter of 1969, another group of students and I, in collaboration with Mr. Theobald, began the preparation of an updated version of this book. Then, quite unexpectedly, the students became so involved (with reasonable success) in the invention of an alternative future for the College itself that the responsibility for the new edition became largely my own. A few students provided valuable help; I wish to thank particularly Deborah Emin, Michael Hart and Jean Markovitz. My primary debt, however, is still to the students who conceived the first edition; it is the conception and organization of that edition which provide the integrity of the second. The original editors and I are also happy to acknowledge our fundamental indebtedness to Kendall College's president, Wesley M. Westerberg, the dean, Robert Thompson, and the faculty, all of whom are sufficiently dissatisfied with the conventional forms of education to allow meaningful experiments, such as our own course, to take place. Finally, we are all gratefully indebted to Robert Theobald, who continues to share his ideas with members of the Kendall College faculty and student body, in person as well as on paper. I hope that the understandings we have gained from his recent thinking on the issues of power and communication will be as helpful to the reader of this new edition as they were to us.

The new materials in this edition are "The Problem," the Addendum to "The Promise," "Inventing the Future," most of "Hunger and Poverty," "Communication to Build the Future Environment," "Ecology: A Dangerous Crusade," "Freedom and Education," Bibliography and the revised Working Appendix. *The revised Working Appendix represents several initiatives brought to our attention since the publication of the first edition. It is our intention to expand this feature of the book as extensively as possible in forthcoming editions, and reader feedback on new initiatives (or worthy old ones) is urgently invited.*

Noel McInnis

Center for Curriculum Design
Kendall College
February 1970

An Alternative Future for America II was further revised in the fall of 1970 when a second printing was necessary. The "Why and How to Dialogue" chapter was added and the Working Appendix was up-dated and expanded.

October 1970

PART I: Here and There

"The priorities of this country are completely out of whack. The generally accepted goals of our society appear to be technological wizardry, economic efficiency and the developed individual in the good society — but in that order.

"We have a socioeconomic system which forces the dehumanization of man. I believe that our first task, therefore, is to begin the restructuring of the socio-economic system to create a human order."

Discussion about the problems and issues of the next decade inevitably opens up a kind of "credibility gap," for any relevant discussion of the next decade will necessarily appear *in* credible. The *appearance* of credibility can only be preserved by failing to challenge the already obsolete conventional wisdom. Such a statement may appear extreme but I believe it to be an excessively sober statement of present reality. The statement's accuracy can be demonstrated both in terms of theory and in terms of the developments of the past decade.

Irving Kaplan, a psychologist who has been much concerned with the impact of computers, has expressed the new situation in the following terms:

"The accelerating rate of technical progress . . . implies three interesting alternatives for the future, each of these alternatives being of a very radical nature.

"The first alternative . . . is that the rate of progress in the technological world of the near future is beyond the comprehension of minds utilizing the contemporary frame of reference. Under this alternative we would not be far from the truth if we predicted that the next twenty years will see far more technological progress than has the previous 2,000,000.

"The second alternative would be a deceleration of technical progress. Such a decline could be due either to the exhaustion of technological potential or to the attainment of such a high level of technology that the culture would be satiated with the technological product and society would shift its values.

"The third alternative would be a catastrophic event such as a disease epidemic of tremendous proportions, a destructive astronomical event, or a war of sufficient destructive force to destroy the nation's or the world's industry and technology.

"Each of these alternatives is so far removed from contemporary experience as to present the individual with a problem of credibility. Whatever direction progress takes from this point on will be a dramatic one."

Because Kaplan's arguments are at a high level of abstraction, it may be helpful to examine the record of the past ten years to see whether recent developments should properly be described as incredible. J. K. Galbraith in *The Affluent Society* argued that there was a gross misallocation of resources: that far too much money was being used for private consumption and far too little was employed in the public sector. The book was rank heresy at the time it was published; it is now accepted. We no longer argue about the need for more money for the public sector; the questions now are "How should the money be raised?" "Where should the limited available funds be allocated?"

The second breakthrough was in the area of poverty. It is often credited to Michael Harrington's book *The*

Other America, for it was Harrington's book that caught President Kennedy's eye and which was the proximate cause of the war on poverty. Today, there is no longer any real argument about the need for special measures to help those who are least able to help themselves. The question is how much money can be afforded and what techniques should be used.

The third change is only now developing but there is every sign that a breakthrough will occur in the foreseeable future. Edward Bellamy proposed in 1887 that a guaranteed income should be provided to each citizen as a matter of right. The public lost sight of this idea until it was revived in my book *Free Men and Free Markets.* In less than five years, the idea moved from being too extreme for almost all thinkers — including radicals — to becoming excessively conventional for those who believe that basic, fundamental change is required. In effect, then, the very course of history smooths over those issues which at one time appeared impossible of solution.

There have been so many changes in our views about the socioeconomy over the last decade that we no longer believe that our views will be stable over the future. We are learning to accept that our growing abundance of material goods and our growing capacity to produce without human toil will require new social and economic arrangements. Indeed, we should perhaps see the most profound change of the last decade in terms of the end of the belief that proposals for changes in the socioeconomic system are heretical.

If proposals for socioeconomic change are no longer heretical, why did I earlier refer to the inevitability of a credibility gap? My reference was due to the fact that although we have come to accept the necessity of *socioeconomic* change, we are not yet ready to accept changes in our view of the *nature of man*. It is this area which will need greater alteration and development in the next decade.

WE MUST CHANGE OUR VIEW OF THE NATURE AND PURPOSE OF MAN

We are engaged in a novel enterprise which requires that we learn to look into the future. In the distant past, men lived and died according to the wisdom of their forefathers and if the wisdom became inappropriate to actual conditions, they vanished from the earth. In the recent past, we have tried to understand the actual conditions which surrounded us and to adapt our system to this reality. We are just beginning to perceive that we must create a socioeconomic system which will facilitate the appropriate education and upbringing for the conditions in which our children and grandchildren will live.

As I have just stated, I am convinced that the most necessary changes are in our view of the nature and purpose of man. Our present institutions and values are based on a highly simplistic thesis which claims that men are moved only by negative and positive sanctions — the whip and the carrot — and that any measures which tend to remove the threat of the whip and the promise of the carrot will contribute to the collapse of the society.

This view is now being challenged by people at the leading edge of most disciplines, perhaps most directly by modern psychology. Modern psychological theorizing postulates that man will strive for self-realization, self-actualization if he is provided with the means to satisfy his more basic needs. It may be helpful to illustrate the immediate consequences and challenge of this new view through a consideration of welfare. If one believes that man can only be moved through positive and negative sanctions, then it is necessary to keep the present welfare apparatus which is still based on poor-law thinking and which tries to force the individual to earn his living through making his condition so unpleasant that toil will appear more attractive. If, on the other hand, man is drawn to the goal of self-realization as his immediate needs are met, then the present welfare system is the *very* factor which is preventing many from realizing their own potential and contributing to the needs of the society.

By extension, the whole debate about the impact of science and technology is coming to revolve around the fact that man needs a personal identity and a purpose in order to decide how the enormous potentials opened up to him personally, and to the society in general, by our growing power ought to be employed. The issue here is that man must gain greater understanding of himself, his personality, his goals and his desires in the coming era, for he will not survive if he is a mere cog in a massive socioeconomic machine.

Such a view is, of course, profoundly antithetical to our present view which is inherited from the nineteenth century and which emphasizes ordered bureaucratic decision-making, within which each individual could be neatly assimilated within a class or group and individual idiosyncrasies could be ignored. But our growing understanding of cybernetics — the science of communication and control — supports modern psychological theorizing rather than the nineteenth-century bureaucratic view.

In this new society, in which men will strive for self-actualization because it *will* be possible to satisfy their lower needs, what changes will be required?

First, we can clearly perceive that we must end, on the one hand, privilege and license and, on the other, powerlessness. In this new society we will have to provide each person with the right to participate in those decisions which affect the environment in which he lives and also with the possibility to affect thinking in any areas where he is willing to take the time and effort to become competent. We are entering a period when an individual's right to affect decisions must depend upon his competence in the particular area in which he is working. It will not be transferable to other areas in which he does not have skills and knowledge.

Second, we can see that the new world will be process-oriented rather than goal-oriented. Western man has always set goals toward which he should strive and has then developed measures to determine whether he was making progress toward his goals. For example, we originally agreed that more goods and services were better than less; we then agreed on rules for measuring the amount of goods and services; and we are now able to say each year that the amount of goods and services available has risen and that we are therefore nearer to our goal of a "high standard of living."

A process-orientation is profoundly antithetical to a goal-orientation. Process means that we determine the progress of an individual or a community in terms of becoming more like its desired pattern. But the extent of movement is inherently unmeasurable both because it is impossible to define clearly what is the desired state of an individual or a community and also because the desired state changes continually. There is no point at which a stop can be put to the process and it can be argued that perfection has been achieved. Process involves uncertainty and risk; a goal-oriented culture essentially tries to eliminate uncertainty and risk although it can, of course, never succeed in doing so.

Third, and intimately connected with each of the last two points, we will come to recognize that each individual is unique and that the overall educational process in which he is engaged throughout his life must help him to realize his uniqueness. This means that we must not impose a set system on any individual, but must rather attempt to provide him with the emotional space in which he can determine his own needs and resources. Our educational system presently fails almost completely to meet the personal needs of the individual for it is designed to turn out people who will fit the systemic requirements of an industrial age which has essentially already ended.

Acceptance of the "uniqueness" of the individual is perhaps part of the rhetoric of today although it is more honored in the breach than in the observance. The corollary of this pattern, however, is seldom mentioned: that it is now possible and necessary to create unique communities. In effect, the industrial age, which was based on production and transportation, required an ever-closer degree of similarity between the various towns and cities in the system so that exchange could be carried through with the greatest facility. We are now entering the information era and this not only allows, but even facilitates, different styles of life. Thus we will be able to encourage unique individuals to discover others with whom they would like to live.

Let me now simply list, with sketch comments, a few of the minimal changes which appear to be essential in the immediate future.

Income maintenance. This framework is the first step toward re-thinking and solving the problems of hunger and poverty and welfare.

Work/Leisure/Education. We must take account of the impact of cybernation on employment. Life could be an unbroken pattern of meaningful activity: no distinction between work and leisure.

Family. The nuclear family is a peculiarly Western industrial-age invention. It likely will not survive the transition from the production-transportation era to the information era which we are entering.

Housing/Environment. The historical necessity for the city has been abolished by the new technologies.

Life/Health/Death. Our decisions about the new techniques which permit the modification of man's body and mind will profoundly challenge all of the practical rules of conduct we have inherited.

This chapter was adapted from a speech originally given during The Shape of the Future Symposium at Yale University, spring 1967.

2 The Alternative

Every period of history has considered itself unique. Nevertheless I believe that those of us who are alive at this moment can make this claim with total confidence, for we have an immediate rendezvous either with unlimited human disaster or equally unlimited human potential. It is the short-run actions of each one of us which will decide the course of history of the world.

During long periods of time, societies and culture are profoundly stable. The actions of individual human beings, or even of large groups, only have marginal effects on their own lives, for the norms within which they live are considered fixed and unshakeable. At certain points, however, a culture ceases to be stable, for its underlying bases cease to be suitable to the changed environment in which it finds itself. At this point, it must either find ways to survive within changed conditions or it must resign itself to collapse.

Arnold Toynbee, the seeker of long-run parallels in culture-history, has argued that cultures confronted with this choice must fail, for they have inevitably lost their resiliency and are unable to deal with the challenge of creatively seizing the opportunities and avoiding the dangers posed by the new environment. Indeed, he argues that cultures will not only collapse but that they have a major tendency to become paranoid: to blame their failures on the activities of outside forces and, in consequence, to use all of their available power to try to crush those whom they come to see as their enemies.

The potential uniqueness of our situation is that we are now sufficiently self-aware to avoid this catastrophic historical pattern. There are two reasons which can compel us to act differently if only we will use our growing knowledge and technological competence. First, the culture which will be destroyed will be our own; if we cannot gain control of existing forces we will be left without any cultural anchors to guide us through our lives. Second, if American and Western cultures should become paranoid — a development which presently seems only too possible — they possess the power to destroy the whole world.

WARNING: The world you destroy is your own

If we can avoid this catastrophic historical pattern, an extraordinary future lies before the human race. The energy we will have available, the knowledge we can create, the computer we can use will make it possible for each man to live in dignity. There will no longer be any necessity to force men to carry out meaningless and degrading tasks, for the machines will be able to do them. There will be no excuse for failing to provide each human being with a right to enough resources to live in dignity. We can afford to spend our lives providing those around us, and ourselves, with the possibility for the fullest development.

The fundamental change in our social system is from the past when it was necessary for man to continue to strive to achieve the power he needed to be able to create the environment he wanted, to the immediate future when it will be possible to do what men wish; but it will be essential to have the wisdom to know what man should wish for himself.

This chapter was originally part of a speech delivered at Washington State University, September 15, 1967.

It is now quite clear that a new view of the nature of man is developing, as many people reexamine the emerging data. This view can be briefly expressed in Abraham Maslow's thesis that human beings begin to drive toward self-actualization as soon as their basic needs for food, clothing and shelter are satisfied.[1] Indeed, there are some suggestions that this insight should be perceived as part of a wider reality — that the universe itself can only be understood in terms of "self-actualization."

POWER AND RESPONSIBILITY DENIED BRINGS ANOMIE OR VIOLENCE

Two major implications would appear to stem from the new insight. First, this convergence among leading thinkers in many disciplines should make it possible to reverse the present, apparently irreversible, trend toward greater specialization.

Second, if it is indeed true that man can only be healthy when he is self-actualizing, it becomes possible to understand many of the developments presently occurring throughout the world which now appear to threaten our survival. Perhaps the most critical of these issues is the demand for power, using slogans such as "black power" and "student power."

At the present time these slogans are widely understood to mean that the groups using them want power without responsibility. In the light of man's absolute necessity to be able to strive for self-development, they take on a different meaning. They state essentially that each man must be provided with the potential to control the conditions of his own life and that the failure to develop this potential leaves him with no choice but to fall into anomie and apathy on the one hand or violence on the other.

It is in this context that today's potential abundance takes on its full meaning: man now has the material ability to provide all human beings with the goods and services required to serve as the basis for full human development. Today, national and international poverty results from a failure of will rather than a failure of productive ability; those who are powerless sense or know this and naturally consider it intolerable.

We have no choice, therefore, but to create a new social order, one where powerlessness has been abolished. For only then will man's drive toward self-actualization be capable of fulfillment and his self-destructive tendencies, generated through failure to honor the fundamental necessity for self-actualization, be eliminated.

[1] See the Addendum below for a summary of Maslow's views on self-actualization. The editors are indebted to Alan Harrod, of St. Mary Center for Learning, for the summary. For additional discussion, see Abraham Maslow's two books, *Toward a Psychology of Being* and *Motivation and Personality*.

Addendum: Maslow on Self-Actualization

Self-actualizing individuals are exceptionally healthy psychologically, being as far in a positive direction from the so-called "normal" personality as the neurotic or psychotic person is in the negative direction. It is Maslow's thesis that the self-actualizing syndrome provides a basis for a theory of psychology oriented toward man's highest potentialities and highest values.

Probably most significant is the self-actualizing person's sharpened perception of reality. He is free from the fears and inhibitions which cause others to distort and cover up a reality which they find too threatening for direct encounter. He accepts himself, others and nature. He has enough self-esteem and confidence to have no need of tearing others down. He is aware of the faults of others, but also of their possibilities and their humanness. He respects the power of natural forces beyond his control and realizes the inevitability of a certain amount of misfortune. He accepts his body and the natural bodily processes without feeling shameful. Thus, the self-actualizing individual in general has an uncommon absence of the fears, frustrations and pressing needs which limit other people's ability to deal effectively and comfortably with their families, friends and acquaintances, and other aspects of the external world.

Related to the above is the pervasiveness of spontaneity and creativity among self-actualizing persons.

They generally feel free to say and to act the way they feel instead of the way others expect them to behave. Although they will modify their reactions when it helps them to be more effective, they are always ready at appropriate moments to toss aside the "cloak of civilization" when no longer needed. Their creativity is defined as a way of life rather than as an ability to produce novel ideas or works. Whatever they do is permeated by an openness, a whimsey and a flexibility very rare among non-self-actualizing individuals. These super-healthy creatures have a continual freshness of appreciation of the little and greater pleasures of living. They shun the contrived "fun" experiences of most cocktail parties and the like, and prefer the first-hand experiences of nature, and meaningful contact with other individuals. A high frequency of ecstatic peak experiences characterizes these persons, as well as the capacity to experience mystical, oceanic feelings of oneness-with-the-universe.

Self-actualizing persons have a quality of detachment and a need for privacy which is greater than that of most people. They no longer need others out of a need for reassurance or to escape loneliness, since they are at peace with themselves and have had previously fulfilling relationships with others. These individuals are highly autonomous and are unusually resistant to enculturation. They can operate within their culture without being intimidated or taken in by it.

Self-actualizing individuals have a democratic character structure which extends to all of their relationships. They are indifferent to class, education, occupation, status and race. Instead, such traits as character, capacity and talents are emphasized. Age and sex differences do not interfere with their acceptance of a person as an individual. They are willing to learn from anyone, but they accept nothing from anyone because of his "position."

An integrated value system is characteristic of people who are self-actualized, their ultimate value being life in general and human life in particular. They may be considered highly ethical people but theirs is not the conventional morality. Self-actualizing persons can differentiate well between means and ends, although they have the ability to enjoy means activities as pleasurable in their own right. Self-actualizing individuals value quality rather than quantity of friendships, and they are capable of extremely deep relationships especially with other self-actualizing persons.

Self-actualizing individuals' attitudes on sex and love vary considerably from what is typical. They can participate wholeheartedly in sexual relations without guilts and without doubts of confidence. If necessary, they can function without sex for long periods without stress and they usually reserve sex for partners they love or for whom they have strong affection. They are sufficiently confident of their masculinity or femininity that they have a much broader interpretation of the sex role than is customary. Love reaches its fullest expression among these individuals, as they do not have the defenses which limit most individuals' capacities to give themselves fully. Yet, although self-actualizing couples can be most totally involved with each other, they allow and even encourage the partner's autonomy and independence, being free of petty jealousies which plague so many couples. They tend to marry individuals who are like themselves in such character traits as honesty, sincerity, kindliness and courage, but such external characteristics as income, religion, nationality and appearance are less important than to more conventional couples. Most remarkably, these healthy persons are intuitively, sexually and impulsively attracted to mates who are rationally right for them.

One of Maslow's most significant conclusions about self-actualizing persons is that these people are capable of resolving the dichotomies considered mutually exclusive by most people in our society. In self-actualizers these polarities disappear by becoming synergic. These people can be both rational and emotional, spiritual and sensual, concrete and abstract, intense and casual, mystic and realistic at the same time, and a thousand problems that confound the normal person disappear. This is not to say that self-actualizing individuals are perfect — they are too human for that. They lose their tempers, get impatient, make blunders, etc., but differ enough from the average for us to question our assumptions about what it means to be homo sapiens.

The change required if we are to survive is to alter our cultural, semantic and psychological patterns. For example, our society conforms to Skinnerian psychology. Professor Skinner developed his psychology from his experiments with animals. He places rats in boxes. At one end of a simple Skinner Box there may be an electric grid, which will give you an electric shock. The rats move off the electric grid because it is unpleasant: the experimenter concludes that rats react to negative sanctions. At the other end of the grid, there is a little lever that can be pushed and food appears. The rats push the lever and they get food: the experimenter concludes that rats react to positive sanctions. The experimenter then generalizes this to apply to human beings, and claims that rats and human beings respond only to positive and negative sanctions.

The best challenge to this theory is to be found in the science fiction story of the Skinner Box psychologist who was caught by an alien race and was put in an alien Skinner Box. He therefore knew exactly what he had to do. Having perceived that it was a Skinner Box, he knew that he had to prove to the alien race that he was intelligent. He also knew that he had to prove that he didn't respond to positive and negative sanctions. So, he explored the box; at one end there was an electric grid. He stayed on the electric grid for some time until it became clear that the alien race would shock him to death. He got off the electric grid, although he realized that he was responding to a negative sanction. At the other end of the cage there was a little lever he could press; he pressed it once experimentally. As he expected, the food came out and he ate it. He then ignored the lever for six days. He got very hungry. Then he started pushing the lever, realizing despondently as he did so that he was responding to a positive sanction. When he had explored the Skinner Box thoroughly, he discovered that Skinner Boxes build into the experimental design what they claim to prove. All Skinner Boxes really show is that sentient beings are not willfully stupid: this is true of rats and human beings.

The average university today is a giant Skinner Box, although nobody meant it to happen this way. If you want a good job, you need good grades. If you want good grades, you need to do well in multiple-choice questions. If you want to do well in multiple-choice questions, you need to keep discrete those nice, attractive, discrete pieces of data you are learning, because if you get them confused you cannot give a simple yes or no answer. It is therefore essential that one does not think, because if you think you get confused.

Supposing you decide that you would like to take the chance of thinking. It is very risky because if you are in a large class, it is impossible for the professor to decide if you are thinking or simply goofing off. And a great many professors do not give you the benefit of the doubt and thus you get very bad grades. If your grades are low enough you go to Vietnam. That is a thoroughly effective Skinner Box.

The argument I get from some professors who claim this analysis is grossly unfair is couched in the following terms: We have, they say, really tried to turn students on. My response is to ask what they mean? "Well," they reply, "one day I went to class and spent forty minutes (or several periods) and I tried to talk to the students and they didn't respond. That proves they need positive and negative sanctions." My further reply is: "These students have been conditioned to such sanctions for anything from eighteen to twenty-two years of their lives. You must give them time to discover new response patterns."

We can break out of Skinner Boxes but we have so far failed to do so. The primary reason we have failed is because our Skinner Boxes were not constructed by ourselves. Indeed, they were not constructed by any individual. They were constructed during an industrial age and were necessary for that age. If we are to break out of our Skinner Boxes we are going to have to work cooperatively. However, in many cases we can just walk out of the Skinner Boxes: the barriers they present are merely perceptions of barriers rather than real barriers. Dean Elizabeth Sewell of Bensalem College at Fordham University says we don't have to wait to get change because basically the institutions have already ceased to exist.

This sounds nonsensical but perhaps I can produce an image which will make some sense of it. Let me suggest to you that we live on a vast plane on which there are a large number of castles. These castles, representing our institutions, are unguarded: the moats are empty and the drawbridges are down. All we have to do is walk into the castles — the old institutions — and take everything out of them that would be valuable for the future. It is necessary to tiptoe in because there are some people who will get mad if you disturb them. So you move quietly. Unfortunately, the people who have been trying to get change up to now haven't been satisfied to tiptoe in and take what they wanted. They have done it in a different way. They assembled outside the castle and they blew their trumpets and claimed they were coming in to take over. The defenders, in a last access of energy, felt challenged to try and defend the castle. Normally, young and vigorous people who want to get change would win the battle, but actually they don't because the castles have installed atomic weapons and the attackers get wiped out.

I believe the reason why people have been unwilling to tiptoe in is their fundamental insecurity. In order for many people to know that they are doing good things they need to be convinced that somebody they dislike believes they are doing bad things. If you are not sure of yourself, the thing you need is a letter from the president of the college which shows he believes you are terrible people. But you believe the president of the college is irrelevant. Therefore if he says you are doing terrible things you must be doing good things.

I am afraid that, in addition, many of the people who

have been attacking the castles are not content to let them decay but would like to see them refurbished with new owners — themselves. They are not looking toward a society without coercive power but rather toward one in which they themselves monopolize the coercive power.

This and the following two chapters were transcribed from informal, extemporaneous talks given at the University of the Pacific and the University of Redlands in March and April, 1968. They remain basically in their initial and informal style.

5 The New Reality

The new reality of today is a very simple one: man now has the power to do what he wants to do. This development is revolutionary because until just this moment of history man has been constrained by his environment. As a result of this novel power, man's present cultural system has become irrelevant, in the same way as man's cultural system became irrelevant when he moved from his hunting and gathering stage to his agricultural stage.

man

has the ability

to provide for all men

The reasons man has this power can be very briefly set out. First, he has power because he has energy, energy being derived today primarily from fossil fuels, but coming tomorrow from nuclear energy. Nuclear energy has the peculiar characteristic that it not only produces energy but in the very process of producing energy it can create more fuel to produce more energy. We are very rapidly getting to the energy potential for a perpetual motion machine. Energy can be used for anything that man wishes — to produce metals from low grade ores, to turn the desert into a garden or whatever it strikes his fancy to do.

The second reason for our power I like to call "alchemy." By that I mean the ability to manipulate the basic building blocks of nature to create materials with the types of properties that one desires. The word alchemy is appropriate for two reasons. It reminds us that some of the materials we have created are already considerably more valuable than gold, and it reminds us of what would happen to the economic system if we simply developed the ability to produce gold. In other words, the economic system is running on a mythology; and the mythology is extraordinarily vulnerable.

The third factor which gives us power is the educational possibilities of our culture. For the first time it is possible for a very substantial proportion of the population to learn for twenty-two years of their lives or more. The fact that we are still running colleges which are largely producing surrogate computers is not the fault of the situation but only the fault of the people within the system. By "producing surrogate computers" I mean that we are educating people who can give answers to questions which have already been posed, which is what a computer can do, rather than teaching them how to pose questions. This is disastrous because the computer will certainly learn to answer structured questions better than we can.

The fourth factor that we have going for us is the computer. The computer is a wonderful instrument.

A computer is a wonderful way of solving problems. But you had better be careful because the computer will give you the "right" answer. This is illustrated in the story about a war planner of a friendly power who asked its computer "What steps should I take to do the most harm to Russia?" The computer, after whirring a few times, came back with an answer, "Bomb the United States." The computer was strictly logical because if this friendly power bombed the United States "intelligently," the U.S. would assume that it had been bombed by Russia. It would then bomb Russia and it could certainly do much more harm to Russia than the friendly power could, because America had more bombs. Theoretically, the great advantage about human beings is that when they see that sort of chasm they stop and say "No, that wasn't what I meant." But computers aren't that sensible.

Using a computer is a good way of getting away from responsibility. We use it in California as a justification for logging redwood groves. The way that this gets done is to instruct the computer to build the best road, and then to inform the computer that the best road is the cheapest road. Next one feeds into the computer the values for the various strips of land, and of course you put in a very low value for the redwoods because, after all, they are not doing any good, are they? The computer then designs a road which goes through the redwood system. Then one says "It wasn't our fault. You know, logic compels us to build the road through the redwood groves. We regret this as much as anybody else."

The computer is a very good servant and a very bad master. There is rather distressing evidence that the computer is becoming a new god. When the computer has spoken, who shall question it? There is no doubt in my mind that the computer has been one of the factors that has led us into the present disastrous situation in Vietnam. I think that everybody now agrees that Vietnam is a disastrous mess. People may disagree about what should have been done or what ought to be done now, but the assumption that errors have been made is common to all of us. One of the factors that got fed into the computer is that the willingness of societies to surrender is a function of the number of bombs dropped on it. Being British I have some grave doubts about this!

Man's new power is not, despite the apparent realities, simply an American or a Western phenomenon. That it can be so limited is one of the great comforting myths. I am asked why I talk about the whole world in these terms. I am told to look at Asia, at Latin America, at Africa, all of whom do not have power. But everybody knows that *mankind* has power. We live, as McLuhan has put it, in a global village. And the fact that some continents do not yet have the power does not prevent them from knowing that they ought to have the power and that they can have the power if the rich are willing to develop it and share it with them.

It would appear at first sight as though a society in which man had power over the conditions of his life would be extremely desirable: indeed, at some level, it is. But this power doesn't mesh with our present social system, and as a result we fall into five very serious traps. The first of these traps is what I call the war trap, the fact that in our international system the ultimate sanction in international dispute is war. Each country must therefore be able to defend itself against any potential attacker, which means that it must install and indeed invent any weapon or defense system that it can. This results in a profoundly unstable world. We have to take the same leap in international affairs as we took in personal affairs some time ago when we abolished dueling. I was taught when I was young that we abolished dueling because people became humane. I have reached the conclusion that this is not true, but that basically people discovered that dueling with modern weapons was too dangerous. Let me point out that we now have available approximately thirty tons of TNT per person, plus enormous destructive potential through biological and chemical weapons. The statement that "war will wipe us out or we will wipe out war" remains as true as it was when it was first stated, but we have numbed ourselves to its reality.

The second trap is the efficiency trap. We run a society in which if something can be done more efficiently, immensely strong forces come into action to ensure change. But the very fact that man has such power over his environment means that he may wish to preserve certain possibilities of human activity which are not efficient. He must therefore change the socioeconomic rules governing international trade and the relationship between income and work.

This can be seen most clearly in relationship to job patterns. In our society everybody must hold a job, unless he is independently wealthy or in a certain very limited group. Computers and machinery are becoming more efficient but men are not becoming more efficient nearly as fast. The efficiency of computers doubles at the present time about every three years, and the cost of computer work probably goes down to one-tenth of its previous cost. At the same time the cost of hiring a worker continues to rise. It is therefore not surprising that a very severe problem of unemployability is emerging. The data are now quite clear: there are more and more people at the bottom of the society who do not have jobs and who are not about to get jobs.

There are only two ways out of this trap. One of them is the idea that the government should become the employer of last resort. That sounds good until you analyze it. What happens when the government becomes the employer of last resort? Some 1,000,000 or more unemployables are placed under the control of federal bureaucrats. These people are unskilled, uneducated, untrained and uninterested in work. The program runs for six months and then Congress wants to know what's going on. It levels charges of inefficiency and lack of control, so the bureaucrats start to tighten up. They pass rules such as: anybody who is fifteen minutes late for work loses a day's pay.

Another rule might be: in order to ensure efficient operation of the system, nobody may change his government-supported job more than once in six months. I would suggest a short word for the result of such rules — an old-fashioned word — slavery. If you think it is an unfair word, I would suggest that you look at some existing national and state welfare policies. The only other alternative is the guaranteed income which says that people are entitled to income as a right and that society has a responsibility to find meaningful work for people to do.

The next trap is the consumption trap, which is related to our productive capacity. If everybody has to have a job we must be willing to consume everything we can produce. We must therefore convince people they should buy. This is particularly visible in our patterns of advertising for children from ages one to five, in an era where television is the prime parent. Television encourages frenetic consumership and permanent debt. "Daddy, Daddy, please buy me . . ."

I said this on TV recently, and somebody said to me, "Well it is really quite all right because children have understood by the age of ten that all advertising is false, anyway." And I said, "You know, if you are right — and you may be right — you have probably explained to me why it is that young people are thoroughly discontented with the society in which they find themselves."

The fifth trap is the education trap. If you have to

bring up people so that they will accept the present traps — the war trap, the efficiency trap, the job trap, and the consumption trap — you dare not set people free to think and study. The educational system ceases to be an opportunity for people to find out for themselves what they believe and becomes a method of manipulating people into accepting what the society currently accepts. It serves as a method for inculcating a set of beliefs from the past which are not relevant to today's world.

We have to understand what has happened to us. We are living in a new generation. This new generation has been brought up within new realities. The people now in college were usually born after the end of the Second World War. Their key realities are basically alien to older people. One of those realities is the fact that the atomic bomb has made international violence impossible in the long run. This rejection of international violence is now causing an understanding that even internal violence must be abolished if we are to survive. The other reality can be best set out in the words of a young colleague of mine: "abundance is a free gift." It is awfully difficult to believe, if one has never done real work as defined by the society, that one is personally responsible for and entitled to that which one has inherited, and to claim that one has produced the food, clothing and shelter needed for his upbringing.

Recognition of the availability of abundance leads to fundamental changes in one's mindset. Psychologist

Abraham Maslow has argued that when people have food, clothing and shelter, they demand to move toward self-actualization and to become more fully human. The first step on this route is a search for a degree of security in their life styles. People are therefore no longer willing to be forced into actions

violence must be abolished
abundance is a free gift

through positive and negative sanctions, or as I prefer, the carrot and the whip. They demand instead the right to develop their lives for themselves in terms of what is meaningful for them. If Maslow is right — and I am convinced that he is — then something fundamentally new has happened. All of the old drives of the human being — drives for food, sex and similar animal drives — are in the process of being replaced by a much higher drive, a drive towards the right to be human.

The new reality entails some very fundamental consequences. If you interrupt this right, if you stop the consequent drives from being realized, you develop the same problems as have existed whenever fundamental psychological drives have been thwarted. The individual is either forced into anomie and apathy, or into violence. I use the word "forced" quite advisedly. It is not a question of "Do you wish to be anomic and apathetic; do you wish to be violent?" Rather, if a human being who needs to be self-actualizing is deprived of any possibility of being self-actualizing, he will become either anomic or violent. For this reason our statements about riots and our statements about student power, black power and poor power make no sense. Society says it deplores the riots, and that it also deplores the conditions which give rise to the riots. If Maslow's theorizing is right, this is nonsensical. We must deplore the fact that society continues to tolerate situations in which human beings are placed in conditions where violence or anomie is inevitable.

The initiative is with us. Are those of us who have the opportunity to be self-actualizing going to use this freedom to find ways to give people power over their own lives, or are we going to continue to do nothing about it? There is a difference between the situation of minorities and the situation of white people. Most of the traps which restrain people who are black or members of other minority groups are real, and no amount of thinking will make them vanish. The basic realities of the inner city are not about to be solved until we change our social systems. On the other hand, the traps in which white people keep themselves are largely of their own making and of their own perpetuation.

The violence and anomie we see around us are symbols of a crisis. But they are not necessarily the harbingers of a disastrous situation. These are the very symptoms which prove that people are ready to change. The very fact that people talk about black power, student power and women power shows that we might be able to live in a free world in which we make our own decisions.

In contemplating the creation of such a world, we must take account of four realities about our present situation. The first and simplest is that the odds are very much against achievement of adequate change. Historian Arnold Toynbee has pointed out that when an environment alters, becoming unsuitable to the culture based on it, the culture collapses: it usually becomes paranoid in the process. (This is a valid description of the present state of American, and indeed Western, culture.) We must recognize that the odds are against change. Those who are engaged in creating change should not be forced to prove they will be successful, rather they must only show that this is the best visible plan at a particular point in time.

Imagine that you are standing at the bottom of a cliff. There is a baby caught on a treetop a hundred feet above you, and the cliff is covered with ice. If you are fully human, the question is not "Do I go up the cliff?" but rather "How do I go up the cliff?" We are entitled to argue, when anybody claims that success is not inevitable, that unless the critic can come up with a better plan we will move as best we know how. It is true that we will certainly know how to do something better tomorrow but we will usually know how to do it better tomorrow because we did it today. Knowledge derives from action as well as intellectual analysis.

The second reality is that people who have been successful within an existing culture are unlikely to be enthusiastic about changing it. The powerless in the existing culture are going to be most interested in change: this means those in minority groups — the poor, the students, women — all those who have been left out of the existing culture. Support for change can also be expected in geographical areas which have not participated in the success of the existing culture. In a very real sense we are now engaged in a struggle between the norms of the industrial culture of the northeast and the rest of the country. But we must be extremely careful not to assume that the correlation is perfect, that all the powerless wish for change and all the powerful are uninterested. This is a particularly important point, because if you assume that a person is not willing to change, he will pick up your attitude and be unwilling to change. People behave much as you would expect them to behave: this provides a prime example of the reality of self--fulfilling prophecy. If you want change, you must assume those with whom you deal also want change, for otherwise they will be uninterested. It is essential that some people with power in our present culture become interested in the possibility of fundamental change, for they alone can solve some urgent problems.

The third reality is related to the second one in a very awkward way. There is no possibility of a revolution if one means by this that one can change totally a set of cultural attitudes. It can't be done.

The more you try this approach the more likely you are to end with exactly the same society as you had when you started. The French and the Russian Revolutions were prime examples of how a culture can survive apparent enormous and total shock with little change. Similarly, it is increasingly clear that the New Left is concerned not to change the present system but to put different people in power; i.e., the ideal is to replace one set of authoritarian personalities with another.

To get revolutionary change be evolutionary

A culture can only be changed in an evolutionary way. The culture must be taken where it is and a new cultural shoot grafted onto it. Essentially, therefore, when you find somebody with an idea you help him develop a better idea which he can feel is still his idea. You can try to get credit for social change, or you can get social change; but you cannot have both. Most of us still want credit for social change and we do not therefore get social change.

Our obvious problem is that powerless people are not very tolerant of the necessity of evolutionary change. Therefore the people who are most willing to bring about change tend to reject the one feasible method of achieving change. The most encouraging recent development, however, is the rapid growth of a "powerless" group who want to find ways to *share power with* the presently powerful rather than demand a mere reversal of roles, with those presently powerless gaining power and those who are powerful losing it.

Perhaps the basic reality, however, is the convergence, coming from many different perspectives, on the need for fundamental spiritual values. We now know that we must develop these values or we will not survive. Let me prove this from cybernetics, the science of communication and control. Cybernetics shows that there are four necessities if any system is to function. The first necessity is that there be accurate movement of information: in human terms this means honesty. The second necessity is that some parts of the system be willing to bring about change when change is needed: in human terms this means responsibility. The third necessity is that no part of the system try to take over the rest of the system: in human terms this means humility.

Gregory Bateson describes our present situation by saying that the worst thing that can happen to a parasite is to find a perfect host. What happens is that the parasite eats the host and then the parasite dies.

Mankind today is a parasite on the environment.

The fourth necessity is that no part of the system try to preserve its exact place in the system but be willing to be flexible as conditions change: in human terms this means love.

Let me point out two further realities in this connection. The first is that American and Western cultures seem as far away from these four necessities for the functioning of a system as any culture has ever been. We presently reject honesty, responsibility, humility and love. But that is only part of the problem. Our need for these necessities is particularly great because of our capacity to destroy ourselves: we can only prevent this when we accept the norms of honesty, responsibility, humility and love.

honesty   **responsibility**

humility   **love**

I have talked about four realities. I would also like to talk briefly about my two key assumptions. My first assumption is that we have something like six to nine months to make visible the beginning of a change from a society of coercive authority to a society of shared power. If conditions continue along present lines, if trends continue to develop as they are presently developing, we will move into a fascist police state in this country. Let me make it clear that I am not arguing that anybody wants a fascist police state. There are few evil men around: our problem is a lack of imagination rather than a problem of evil. We are being forced toward a fascist police state by events and we will continue to be forced by events unless we change our attitudes. The fact that the development of such a police state will be unwilled does not make it less real.

My second assumption is that there has been a mutation in Western man: that most of us would earnestly like to be human. Unfortunately, we are unwilling to admit that we are really human and that we really don't like the roles we are presently compelled to play. Thus we go around today wearing carefully designed masks that we have developed with great care during our lifespan. These masks prevent us from knowing each other. They prevent us from actualizing the profound truth announced by the Beatles, that we can get by with a little help from our friends.

I believe that most of us would like to learn to destroy our masks. All we have to do is to start to take them off, demonstrating that we would like to be human with other human beings. Our problem is not in somebody else. It is not the bad other guy, it is us. Our problems come from our inabilities to live our own lives with wisdom and courage, our own inability to think through the problems with which we are faced. We must therefore announce to the world, to quote Pogo: "We have met the enemy and they are we."

Again I make the central assumption that our society and our world are going to learn what it means to be self-actualizing, that we will no longer need to use the whip and the carrot to move people. When this occurs we will be able to set people free to do what they believe is important to themselves and to other human beings.

What is the meaning of this statement? There are two levels at which it can be explained. At one level it is necessary to state that if you don't know, I can't tell you. This, however, is an unsatisfactory answer, although it is not a trick answer since some realities can only be discovered by participation. I believe, however, that one can state some of the characteristics of self-actualizing human beings. One key factor is that self-actualizing people are so sure of themselves that they do not need to hurt another human being to know they exist. One reason we cause pain to other human beings is because it shows we are alive: we're forced to create pain because we're not creative enough to create joy. Today we no longer seem to believe that "I think, therefore I am." Rather, too many of us say, "I cause pain, therefore I am." This can now be changed to "I feel, therefore I am." An individual who has sufficient surety of his own existence does not need to prove he exists by hurting other individuals.

The second key factor is that an individual who is self-actualizing is unique. Americans have been trained not to exhibit any depth of character: it is very easy to get to know quickly the masks they have developed. The European I was brought up with was rather like an onion. Each time you met him you peeled another layer off. You cried a lot, but it was always interesting. A self-actualizing human being will be sufficiently interesting that you can spend the rest of your life trying to get to know him or her.

However, I suspect that this idea of the ever-interesting person will force us to abandon the concept of the nuclear family, i.e., husband, wife and children. Such an abandonment does not rule out monogamy, which has existed for centuries in cultures which have a variety of forms of the extended family. It appears to be unrealistic to expect two grown people to play all the roles required for a full, developing life. The idea that one can find everything that one needs in one other person, without other close relationships, is a tragic distortion of the meaning of community. We need to develop a very wide range of diverse communities.

Once we accept the potential of diversity, most of the questions that we ask become nonsensical. We try to discover what the new world is going to be like, but by definition the new world won't have a single reality. There will be unique individuals and diverse communities: every generalization will therefore be false. Acceptance of the idea of a self-actualizing individual actually results in a drive towards many different communities in which people can maximize their potential to become themselves.

Several critical questions are raised at this point. First, what about mobility? Many people have argued that the degree of mobility can be used to measure the level of civilization. I disagree. It seems to me that the amount of travel we will carry out in the future will be greatly reduced. This will occur because we will not want to leave our friends, and because we will have the technological capacity to create varying environments within a given community. The technology will be ready when we have decided what we want.

The second question is in terms of the way we will bring up children. In the world of the future is it possible for children to grow up to emotional maturity in the same environment in which they were born, or must they move? I know no answers to this question, but I'm quite convinced it is a very real, genuine issue.

Third, how are people to change from one state in their life pattern and develop to another, from being a young person to an adult, from being unmarried to married? Our society does not dramatize changes in life style. Weddings, for example, have become just a vestige of what they were and many persons are very impatient even with the vestige. We must examine once more whether we need to dramatize changes in the situation of the person.

Fourth, we must reconsider the implications of our complete destruction of all celebrations. We have a

lot of holidays, but they are not community celebrations in any sense. They are simply opportunities
to go to the beach, etc. Does a living and vibrant
community require some occasions on which it meets
together and celebrates the fact that it exists as a
community? Again, I don't know an answer, but I do
think it is a very real, urgent and important question.

There will, I believe, be one common thing about
communities just as there is one thing common to all
individuals. The community will be diverse but will
always involve a living, learning experience. Life will
essentially be learning. In the 1970's we will create
genuine learning communication centers in the home.
One will be able to call up facts, figures and all the
data required for the solution of his problems. The
potential of cable television is extremely interesting
here, because it provides much of the technology for
a communications city.

life will essentially
be learning

We will combine the university and the community.
There appear to be two key requirements in effectively combining universities and communities. One is
the existence of a well-designed, efficient communication center. This will provide information about

what is going on in the community at any given moment of time, and will also enable one to find out who in the community is interested in the same issues that he wishes to work on. This involves an intellectual analog of Operation Match, and can be programmed on a computer. The second requirement is a first-class, person-to-person, portable telephone system. This scares some people but I cannot understand why. I can think of nothing better than having my telephone with me if certain technological capabilities are built into it. In effect, you need to be able to express your willingness to receive telephone calls.

There could be three levels of willingness to take calls. The first level would be: "I'm not doing anything important and I'm quite willing to accept a call from anybody." The second level would be: "I'm busy and I do not wish to be disturbed; however, if it is urgent, you can call me." The third level would be: "I'm not to be disturbed except in an absolute emergency." Equipment would also be available to record messages. This proposal is not beyond our technical capacity if we should start putting as much effort into community actions as we have into sending people to the moon.

The person originating the call must have the right to determine whether he will put through the call: there are always certain things we all want to know immediately, regardless of what we are doing. For example, one would want to know if one's wife, mother or husband were ill.

Diverse communities would move rapidly toward a free goods situation: one where a person walks into a store and takes whatever he wishes off the shelves. We may not have reached a free goods situation by the end of the 1970's but we will certainly have moved a long way towards it. This is inevitable because an increasing number of people will be living on Basic Economic Security (BES) and Committed Spending (CS). People who live on BES and CS are not going to use money for exchanging goods among themselves. They are going to swap human services without exchanging money.

The availability of free goods would lead to some very interesting developments. First, we could begin to eliminate the power which has been accorded by the community to certain groups in the society, which enables them to peg high prices, rates of interest, wages and salaries. In the future, prices, wages, rates of interest and salaries should fall because prices would be related to scarcity and we are moving into a position of abundance. Second, as people can choose to move out of jobs they dislike into areas of activity which seem good to them, because of their possession of BES and CS, wages and salaries available for pleasant jobs would start to decline. Because of this decline in wages and salaries, it would become less attractive to spend money inventing and installing machines to replace pleasant areas of work. At the other end of the spectrum, the first result of a guaranteed income would be to force people to pay an adequate wage for unpleasant jobs.

No one would do unpleasant jobs unless he got paid an adequate wage for it. The consequent rise in wages would make it attractive to automate and thus eliminate the jobs that people don't want to do.

This combination of forces would move us towards a system of free goods. A theoretical analysis of this necessity has been developed. It was created by a non-economist, which is perhaps not surprising. The argument is essentially very simple. It is first demonstrated that we are moving beyond the point where work is unwanted. If work is pleasant, why should we pay somebody to act in ways which are attractive to him. In addition, we are moving to the point where the overall supply of goods could be adequate if we were not bedazzled into buying things we don't need, thus increasing our sensory overload. In these circumstances, where work is attractive and consumption available, the old methods for distributing income are no longer valid: the only possible route is to provide each person with the option to work as much as he likes and to consume as much as he wishes.

We are reaching the point where we understand that too much is not better than too little: we are realizing the virtue of balance. We are moving towards a situation in which we will choose to dress and eat rather plainly, but attractively, for the most part. Occasionally we will go out and have a wonderful time. But we won't do it very often because it isn't really worth doing very often.

If you travel on expense accounts, you get tired of "good dinners" pretty soon. I usually travel on an expense account of some sort. I can eat anything and anywhere I want to. But I very seldom eat in the expensive restaurant in the hotel. I go to the coffee shop. Let me therefore sound really far out by suggesting that within ten years, maybe by the end of the 1970's, we will have a new style of restaurant serving the best food. The only way you will be able to get into it is by going dressed in your very best and being happy enough for other people to enjoy your being there. I know we can't imagine a society of this type but then you couldn't "imagine" our present system: it is much too improbable!

We can't even "imagine" our present system

How does one make decisions in a community containing self-actualizing individuals? One employs the task force system presently employed by business. This brings together the people who have the competence to solve particular problems, and the organization accepts that the solutions will be the best possible. This technique could be applied in communities today if trust existed. But it does not. In this area, therefore, as in every other, we must create trust. However, once we have realized the implications of self-actualization, the problem will cease to be important for we have already seen that such a person does not need to hurt another to prove he exists, and groups of self-actualizing persons will always try to develop the best possible solutions to problems.

The task force pattern eliminates the classical political problem of who shall guard the guardians. In this model the guardians guard the guardians because an imaginative, creative person cannot tolerate a destructive person. Among creative, synergetic people, the authoritarian, destructive personality stands out like a sore thumb. The people in the group will rapidly exclude any person who refuses to become a member of the decision-making group unless he can run the group.

Task forces of this type create reality. But only those involved in the process can really understand what happened. It is meaningless to ask how something developed if one was not present: indeed this question may be unanswerable even if one was present because the most critical interactions may have seemed unimportant.

(People come up to me after we have had task force sessions and say "I had a real urge to say something." I ask, "Why didn't you?" And they say, "Well, I wasn't sure I should speak." My reply is, "It's up to you to determine the dynamics. Maybe what you didn't say is precisely what needed to be said.")

I think we will have two essential levels of government. One will be local and involved in immediate decision making. The other will be international. We will be well on our way towards such a reorganization by 1980. The international decisions will be in terms of removing limitations and facilitating opportunities relative to what people desire to do locally.

Proposals for such thoroughgoing reorganization of society may seem impossible. I believe that those people who argue about impossibilities do so because they have not looked at the available technological potential. The studies by R. Buckminster Fuller show our capacity to produce not only for the United States and the rich countries but for the world. The poor countries of the world do need an infinitely greater amount of goods and services than the rich countries could provide immediately, even if a total commitment were made. But all plans for massive provision of resources assume that one simply dumps in goods and services, techniques and technology, without worrying about the cultural impact; that we already know how to give aid to other countries without wrecking their cultures. It seems to me that such assumptions are invalid. We can therefore commit ourselves to creating a human society in the United States and still take on an unlimited commitment to provide the poor countries with all the help they can culturally afford to absorb.

The gross national product of the United States can grow by about forty billion dollars a year in real prices. The total amount of foreign aid to all countries, which is mostly military aid, is not more than ten billion dollars. Even if one assumes an increase in foreign aid by 50 per cent a year — which is a heroic assumption — this does not cut very far into the potential increase in the United States gross national product. (You will note that I have based my figures on the new levels of increase in production we could reach.)

I would propose that we work towards an international synergetic decade of the seventies. The 1960's were called the development decade. It flopped. It was meant greatly to increase the amount of growth in the poor countries but the record shows that the rate of growth was slow. During the international synergetic decade, people should think and work together to provide enough food, clothing and shelter for everyone. We should be ready to launch this decade in 1970, and should have the resources and intellectual commitment to carry it through at this point. We should resolve as persons, not as governments, that by the end of the 1970's each human being in this world would have enough food, clothing and shelter to live with some dignity.

I think this is an achievable goal. For example, the biggest food problem is a lack of protein, and we have the skill to mass-produce protein at low cost. The problem is similar to that involved in wiping out poverty in the states. It is a question of will. The issue before us is whether we will use our brains and our intellects and our emotions to solve our problems and create our potentials. We can all continue to say we are only churchmen, or only educators, or only students, or only government people — that our role is limited, and that we cannot be expected to solve the problems of the world. But the job of world-problem-solvers has not yet been allocated. Some of us had better choose to define ourselves as world-problem-solvers if world problems are going to be solved.

some of us had better
choose to define ourselves
as world-problem-solvers

My basic invitation is to get into the business of being world-problem-solvers. However, I would hope you would play this role with two things firmly in mind. The first is that we know very little indeed: well over 90 per cent of what passes for knowledge and wisdom is false. If you assume that simply because someone is a teacher, or a businessman or a member of the government, then he must know more than you know, our chances of getting intelligent solutions are very low. The second thing to keep in mind is that we can only move in terms of our own knowledge, which is limited but which can be increased by listening to the people around us.

We need a peculiar mix of pride and humility. We must work with people, but we must also trust our own judgment. In the end, things must make sense to me: there is nobody who can take me off the hook of making my own final decisions about meaningfulness.

We are in a crisis. We can continue to say that somebody else is going to solve our problems. The evidence is now clear that in reality nobody is going to solve our problems. Will we act to solve our own problems? The choice is ours.

PART II: Getting There

"I have developed an analogy about a train running on tracks headed over a cliff. Many of us are fighting to get at the controls. But the control board does not slow the train down. The only significant act, therefore, is to jump off that train, come together, get a helicopter, and leap far enough ahead of the train to lay a new set of tracks which leads away from the cliff.

"The analogy is, I think, a useful one. It says several things. It says that we are very unlikely to succeed. It also says that so long as one is on the train one cannot be truly significant — that we can fight any number of battles on that train, but they are not going to make much difference to the end result; and that it is only in designing and laying a new course — or in my analogy, a new set of tracks — that man can survive."

As some of you know, I have flown for about fifteen hours to reach this conference and I now face the thought of another fifteen hours flying to get back to my temporary home in the south of France. Those of you, who, like me, suffer from excessive travel will recognize that there must be some powerful reasons which brought me here.

Let me start with the geographical reasons. I am not one of those who thinks that the truly important decisions are being taken in the Northeast United States. Rather I believe that the decision-making centers in New York, Washington and Detroit are devoted to shoring up a culture which is clearly collapsing.

Decision-making centers in America
are moving away from the Northeast

It has been argued by Arnold Toynbee that those who were successful in a particular period of history cannot reasonably be expected to perceive the need for change as conditions alter and that they must therefore be expected to operate with techniques and rules which are no longer valid. My experience confirms this insight and I therefore believe most strongly that if we are to deal with the crisis we so clearly face we will do so on the basis of actions taken by the "periphery" rather than by the "center."

My second reason for coming is that it is now urgently necessary that we clarify the directions in which we can move if life on this planet is to continue into the twenty-first century. It is my firm conviction that most "futurists" in our society are still justifying obsolete industrial-age values rather than trying to clarify the minimal requirements for our survival as we move from the industrial era based on power, competition, production and transportation to the cybernetic era based on cooperation, process and information movement.

It is true that more and more development consultants insist that production and transportation are becoming less and less important and are being replaced by the information industries. However, these same development consultants typically fail to understand that the methods of creating and developing the information industries are necessarily profoundly different from those valid for the production and transportation industries. My main purpose here will be to sketch the nature of the issues involved in creating a socioeconomy in which information movement is dominant and to suggest briefly how the states and provinces in the Northwest portion of the North American continent can take advantage of this emerging socioeconomic system.

NATURE OF PROGRESS

These introductory comments will probably have

been sufficient to inform you that I do not belong to the dominant liberal intellectual majority in this country. It is an article of faith within the liberal elite that existing trends can be expected to continue, that such changes as occur will be minor and that the world in the year 2000 will be a larger, flashier, but still recognizable, version of the world of the year 1969.

This view is based on the fallacy that continued progress is possible, that the basic current trends can be expected to continue at least as far as the year 2000 without important change. This is the assumption in the work of Herman Kahn, the most prominent of existing futurists, as well as in the work of the Commission on the Year 2000.

Those who deal with the real world are well aware that the only pattern which can be ruled out for the year 2000 is the one that is recognizable in terms of the year 1969. After all, 1938 provided a bad base for predicting socioeconomic norms in the year 1969. I would therefore be engaging in rhetorical overkill if much time was spent dealing with this point. However, for any who need conviction, let me suggest that an examination — at even the simplest level — of the environmental/ecological/population issue makes it clear that we shall either perceive the issue in a totally new way by the year 2000 or the planet will be under sentence of death through man's own stupidity. The extensive resources of the Northwest in the environmental resources field makes it critical that this rethinking begin here immediately.

Martians, I assume, like scorched earth.
They can come and have this planet
in some twenty years, unless . . .

Dennis Gabor, the British physicist, provides us with an elegant theoretical reason for the abolition of the doctrine of progress. "In today's world all curves are exponential. It is only in mathematics that curves grow to infinity: in real life they either break down catastrophically or gently." It is our duty as thinking men to strive toward a gentle saturation. In other words, if we should sustain the progress doctrine, catastrophe is inevitable; however, we can only under-stand — let alone accept — the idea of gentle satura-tion *after* a fundamental change in values.

A rational computer analysis of our present situation would undoubtedly conclude that we shall fail to change our attitudes and values in time. I could easily demonstrate the likelihood of this reality and thus help to create a self-fulfilling prophecy. I prefer, however, to assume that we have perceived the need for change; I wish to discover how best it can be brought about.

Given the fact that one can only think within world views which have been invented, what alternative futures are presently being advanced? The most widely cited analysts today have returned to an older view: that the world is based on a circular flow and that the cycles of activity eventually return to their starting point. In this view there is truly nothing new under the sun. Marshall McLuhan, for example, argues that the industrial era was only a break between two essentially similar periods and that we are now returning to tribalism.

This circular view is, of course, anathema to those who believe in progress; it is for this reason that McLuhan has been so widely attacked by those who foresee the continuation of present views and values. I believe, however, that his central point is correct: that we have no option but to decentralize. McLuhan challenges the belief that we can further divide current tasks and still demand of people that they act as ever more efficient cogs in an increasingly complex machine. McLuhan claims that we are going to be forced to recognize the individuality of each person, the uniqueness of his development and the need for diversity in communities and institutions if each person is to be able to develop his potential. This stress on uniqueness is now developing at the leading edge of both the physical and the social sciences; it is no longer an unusual theme.

But while I believe McLuhan is correct in his belief about decentralization, I find his idea of circularity incorrect. We cannot go through the same experience twice, for the world will always have changed. Man has moved from being part of the natural environment to being able profoundly to affect the natural environment. In effect, therefore, we must *combine* the view that progress is inevitable if life is to continue with the view that life is circular. When we do so we see that life should be viewed as a series of spiral staircases. Human history has been a series of upward steps to higher levels of consciousness during which we have passed through similar patterns of social organization.

It is indeed true, for example, that there are only a limited number of possible life styles — for example, family organization can only be handled in a limited number of ways. However the effect of a basic pattern of family life will be profoundly different depending on the level of technology which has been achieved: consider the extended family with and without the possibility of efficient contraception. A "tribalized" society with high levels of technology cannot possibly operate similarly to the tribal culture of earlier periods where tools were still "person-operated."

Some may feel that a discourse on conflicting world views is interesting but somewhat too high-flown for the purpose of this conference, which is to find ways to plan the future of the Pacific northwest. Let me therefore state just one of the implications which stems from these differences. Those who believe in continued progress argue that we must make room for the development of huge, homogeneous megalopoli whose presumed physical ugliness can only be matched by their hideous suggested names: Boswash, Chidet, etc. Those who disagree argue that we must anticipate large numbers of unique small communities linked by communication rather than transportation. Those who perceive life as "spiral staircase" state that it is only if the total society learns to organize itself around communication rather than transportation that survival in small communities will be possible. We must plan for one of these options; we cannot straddle them, we must choose. To do so we must get a sense of the process which has occurred during the 1960's.

POWERLESSNESS OF "POWER"

The conventional view of the sixties is that they were born in hope and that they died in despair. Historically, however, the sixties will be seen as the period in which man succeeded in defining the nature of the new problems/possibilities he had created through his own actions; and, through his increased self-awareness, began to learn how to avoid the disasters which now seem almost inevitable.

(I am assuming, of course, that there will be a future from which historians will be able to look back on the sixties. This must be seen as an act of faith, for the most probable course of events is the ending of human life on earth, whether through nuclear holocaust or environmental pollution. However, it is in part the very certainty of this ending, if man fails to become creative, which gives us reason for hope.)

Effective action to deal with crises is only possible when one understands them and has discovered the problems and possibilities which are inherent in the critical situation. So long as one feels surrounded by a multitude of unrelated, incoherent events, it is impossible to do more than react to each event with ad hoc solutions which only too often aggravate the situation even in the short run, let alone over a lengthy period of time.

Today it is clear that the vast majority of the population feel that they are surrounded by a set of mutually reinforcing crises. However, it is possible to understand them as part of a single critical reality. This critical reality can perhaps be most easily understood if we reverse one of the best known political aphorisms and argue that in today's world "Diplomacy is the continuation of war by other means."

DIPLOMACY IS THE CONTINUATION OF WAR BY OTHER MEANS

What does this imply? In the nineteenth century and the early twentieth, it was believed that when reason failed war was a "logical" next step. Today, however, war can solve nothing, for the use of all available force would destroy the world. Total war is impossible. Once total war has been ruled out, war becomes a communication medium about the determination of the participants and their willingness to endure, rather than a sure means of eventual victory or defeat. (This statement probably applies only where one of the "great" powers is involved; however, in today's interconnected world, there are few areas where this is not the case.)

It is for this reason that the Vietnam war has proved so confusing for all concerned. The United States could win the war at any point by using some of its most destructive weaponry, but the costs for the future of the world order are too high to be acceptable. The use of available force would probably make more enemies than friends both internally and internationally. In these circumstances, the Vietcong and North Vietnamese cannot lose the war but they too make enemies by their military activities and the cost of enduring is so high that talks make sense for them also. It is for this reason that the discussions in Paris started; it is our mutual inability to discover the implications of this new world where "power" is no longer effective which delays the conclusion of the talks.

While we have begun to perceive the reality of change in power relationships internationally, we have not yet really started to understand that the same development is occurring domestically. It goes without saying that the government has the force to destroy totally any group of protesters by depriving them of rights essential to a meaningful life in the twentieth century; heavy-handed action, however, makes friends for the protesters. Similarly, protesters have the force to destroy effectively any institution which displeases them, but excessive use of such force is clearly counter-productive to any goal of achieving meaningful change.

Many governments throughout the world hold a veto power on human history: they have the power to destroy the world. In addition, many institutions and protesting groups have it in their power to prevent favorable developments; destructive force is widely shared and can be exercised by a few people. However, avoidance of chaos and breakdown can *only* be achieved, both internally and internationally, if all groups strive together to discover what must be done to create the future.

In one sense, the threat we confront is not new, for cultures have collapsed many times in the past because of their refusal to permit new and dynamic groups to be involved in the re-creation of the society. This unwillingness led to a withdrawal of consent-by-the-governed, a gradual weakening of the society and an eventual take-over of the society by an outside group. In today's conditions, however, failure to involve dynamic groups will be totally disastrous, for it will ensure the end of human history, either by holocaust as the underprivileged try to exert power against those with nuclear weapons, or in chaos as man refuses to adapt to new conditions.

The multiple crises by which we are afflicted are the visible symptoms of a potentially deadly disease. Today we are attempting, at best, to cure the symptoms and, at worst, to suppress them because they make us uncomfortable. We cannot expect to see any systemic improvement until we discover how man can learn to choose wisely.

Our failure to evaluate imaginatively the meaning of our new situation is made all the more dangerous because we have failed to recognize that the American people are ahead of their leaders in reevaluating the world. There is a movement against all sources of power which do not justify their actions. This ranges from anger against black and campus militants through reaction against the foundations to distrust of the Pentagon. However, in the absence of a new fundamental understanding of the world in which we live, there is a clear-cut tendency to describe present trends as indicative of a simple movement to the right — and in so describing them to create a repressive movement against urgently needed social change.

President Nixon claimed in his inaugural address that one major hope for the country was to provide all citizens with an opportunity to take part in planning for their future. In the light of the analysis above it is clear that the President was right. It is difficult, however, to perceive any major effort to translate this into reality. The problem is made all the more difficult because no activity of this type can succeed unless it starts at the grassroots and works upwards to

Washington through communications channels rather than starting in Washington and working downward through existing control channels.

We have developed the techniques which could be used to involve the citizen. For example, it is quite possible to create a series of activities based on the combination of mass-media diffusion of ideas and small-group discussion of these ideas, thus giving each citizen the opportunity to learn enough to cast meaningful political ballots. Local experiments throughout the United States and Canada, most recently that of the Stone-Brandel Center in Chicago,[1] have proven the validity of the technique. All that remains is to achieve a commitment equal to the magnitude of the task.

COMMUNICATION PATTERNS: DEDUCTION/INDUCTION

True communication requires trust between those taking part in the discussion. It is made effectively impossible by one of the dominant realities of the past and the present: the desire to divide the world between "we" and "they." Both animals and men mark off the territory belonging to their group and attempt to enforce respect for these boundaries. While the passage of time has led men to enlarge the physical area and number of people comprised in "we", the belief that "they" are evil remains largely unchanged.

Man's achievement of essentially unlimited power requires that he alter this pattern. We must adopt

Pogo's the-enemy-is-we wisdom. Given the fact that
our power is now so great that we no longer dare use
it, our only hope is to learn to communicate to solve
our differences. This requires that we cease to exclude "them" from the human race.

"We have met the enemy
and they are we"

Unfortunately, however, the needed patterns of communication are profoundly different from those
which exist in the industrial age. Young people often
claim that older people do not understand them and
older people often claim that the young are incapable
of thinking clearly. In a very real sense both groups
are right, and it is this "rightness" which causes high
levels of tension. The definition of the word "communication" is not in fact compatible for the two
groups.

Most — but of course not all — older people believe
that the appropriate goals for the society are known
and that the proper task of meetings and discussions
is to discover how best to achieve these goals. In these
circumstances it is possible to proceed by deduction
to discover the "one best way" to carry out a particular task or to reach a particular goal. Deductive
thinking is based on logic and clarity. Those who have

learned deductive thinking find that the young think fuzzily, for they will not adhere to the agenda. In fact, the young are trying to challenge the agenda for they find it takes too much for granted.

Many young people — and particularly those likely to be involved in discussing social issues — argue that the goals presently accepted by the society are inappropriate for our new circumstances. In other words, there have been system breaks. Their struggle to define the implications of the system break necessarily involves induction, with its implied necessity for the temporary acceptance of uncertainty in goals. They feel that the old prevent any significant discourse from developing.

Induction clashes profoundly and deeply with deduction and with the established life styles of the culture in which we live. Induction has two critical characteristics. First, the inductive process cannot occur when those involved in it concentrate on the word, phrase, sentence or paragraph of the individual who is talking. Rather, it is necessary for all those involved to listen for the sense that the individual is trying to put across. (The word "trying" is of key importance here, for the individual is not engaging in induction if he is fully clear what he is talking about. It is only when he is somewhat out of his depth that he is truly seeking new levels of understanding.) The task during the process of induction is to grasp the sense of the statements made by oneself and others, and to attempt to discover what new truths can be developed together.

Second, one must recognize that people are not willing to show the vulnerability of their lack of knowledge except in a situation where trust exists. If, therefore, there is not a psychic basis for trust between the members of the group there can be no real inductive discourse. It is for this reason that the presence of a single individual who does not believe in the need for induction can prevent the development of induction. The effectiveness and success of inductive reasoning cannot be proved, it must be experienced. The minimum requirement for such an experience is the suspension of disbelief.

The existing clash between inductive and deductive methods must inevitably lead to tensions. The level of tensions is augmented beyond the obvious because of two factors. One is that there is little real understanding of the causes of ineffective communication; there is therefore a tendency to assume that it is due to the evil of "them" rather than to a lack of understanding. In addition, the conflict is sharp because the presently dominant deductive style which caused the industrial revolution is now being undermined by the inductive style clearly required in the communications era which we are now entering. This change from the dominance of deduction to the dominance of induction threatens many in the society.

It may be valuable to translate this theoretical reasoning into forces which impinge on apparently powerful individuals. The people who presently appear to control our society are usually male and between forty-five and sixty-five. Many of them feel threatened in three key ways. First, the values defined as male in Western culture — those of force and competition — are being replaced by those values which have been defined as feminine in Western culture — those of process and cooperation. In these circumstances a large part of the male self-image appears challenged.

Second, it is increasingly obvious that given the present pace of change, it is inevitable that young people will know more in certain areas than the old. Thus the pattern which has applied almost everywhere in human history of the old informing the young is giving way to a far more equal relationship.

Third, many people in our culture are now afraid of losing their jobs either to well-trained young men or to computers. Even if people feel secure in their posts they are threatened in a more subtle way, for the effect of the computer and new styles of management is to prevent them from exercising true decision-making power.

In these circumstances, many of those who now hold positions of apparent power feel very severely threatened. They strove to gain the power to give orders and to have them obeyed. Now that they have reached the positions toward which they strove, they find themselves to be but one element in a communications net which can be influenced but cannot be controlled; indeed the harder they strive to control it the more inefficiently the system comes to operate. Many of those who wanted to have power find the reality intolerable, and they therefore attempt to convince themselves that nothing significant has changed. The inductive style of young people — which is inherently aimed at a reconsideration of the total situation — is therefore profoundly threatening, for it challenges all those involved to reexamine an area which they have attempted to close off.

NEW BASIS FOR POWER

Tom Paterson, a Scottish management consultant, has argued that there are two forms of authority: structural and sapiential. Structural authority is that which derives from one's position; one has the right to command because one holds a certain rank or title. Those who use structural authority act as though the question "Why" has no relevance. For them it is sufficient to reply "Because I say so." Failure to obey results in force. This is held to be justified simply because there was a refusal to obey, however ridiculous the order may have been. A combination of forces is meeting to destroy the validity of structural authority. The most important of these is the growing inability to use force without negative results.

It is not an exaggeration to state that the major cause of the present crisis is a universal movement away from the acceptance of structural authority. A substantial part of the highly visible revolt against the military is due to their unwillingness to explain their reasoning and their tendency to propagandize (or to use a blunter Anglo-Saxon term: to lie) when caught in an untenable situation. Presidents of colleges, governors of states and presidents of nations who try to use structural authority also find their credibility vanishing.

SAPIENTIAL AUTHORITY

We are so used to the idea of power being based on structural authority that we fear its end, for we suspect that chaos may result. But there is another form of authority which Tom Paterson calls "sapiential." This is authority based on knowledge and which emerges through true communication. Sapiential authority can, and will, justify its decisions; for those using it the proper response to the question "Why" is an explanation of the reasoning which led to the decision and a modification of the decision if the reasoning ceases to be valid, either because of intelligent questioning or for other reasons.

As I have already stated, the American people are coming to distrust structural authority. They increasingly desire that the decisions to which they are subject should be explained. It would take too long to give examples from every area, but let me take just one which is well-known. There have been several flare-ups between the astronauts and the ground-crews. This has been due to the fact that the astronauts have clearly felt that the ground controllers were trying to make decisions based on rank when the astronauts' situation gave them, and only them, the sapiential authority necessary.

What then of the policies necessary for the future? I see no present revolt against sapiential authority, even when the holder of sapiential authority possesses structural authority as well. (I recognize that a small, vocal and tragic group believes that the world can be run without authority of any sort, but I am convinced that attention will move away from this group as we develop a viable strategy for change.) I would suggest, therefore, that the prime requirement is to find the means of moving rapidly away from our present socioeconomy which is based on the use of structural authority toward one based on sapiential authority.

POLICY SUGGESTIONS

Let me now draw out some of the conclusions which result from the theses that we must move from structural authority to sapiential authority and from an emphasis on production and transportation to an emphasis on information creation and movement. What should you do? The answer to this question must be specific in part, for the possible range of your futures emerges from your past history and present geography; it must be general in part, for it must emerge from dreams which all will come to share. Let me give three examples. Because I make these suggestions while standing in the Pacific Northwest, I partially slant their specificity in that direction, but they are equally relevant for all Americans.

The most obvious step is that you should serve as a bridge to Asia. But this should be done as a sort of reverse foreign aid. Up to the present time, we have been exporting both our Western technical know-how and, together with it, a set of values which are clearly far from appropriate to the real conditions of tomorrow both for ourselves and for the poor countries. It seems, on the contrary, very possible that much of the fundamental Asian philosophy is relevant to our present conditions, where man needs primarily to control his power through communication rather than to increase it. The prime problem, of course, will be to find scholars who have not completely swallowed the Western doctrine of progress, but who can nevertheless relate to its benefits as well as criticize its faults.

Second, you can lead in the long-overdue movement for university reform which must inevitably emerge on the periphery. Those in the prestige universities are too caught up in the intellectual power structures of today to recognize their own obsolescence. We must start by reexamining the purpose of the university. The university today is a monstrosity which has grown like Topsy and without thought or consideration. Both school and university act to cut the child off from the real world, to provide him with data which all too often have no relevance except to achieve a diploma or a degree. In addition, and increasingly, schools serve to keep the individual off the labor market which could not absorb him. Finally, and most seriously, the school and university operate, almost entirely, on the basis of structural rather than sapiential authority. It is this latter reality which is at the heart of much current protest.

Considered analytically, the undergraduate university consists of two primary groups: students who are there because they must ingurgitate, for later regurgitation, the facts required for their degree; and professors who prefer research rather than teaching undergraduates. These two largely antipathetic groups are held together by three myths: first, that students cannot be involved in the creation of knowledge until they have understood all that has been previously learned about the topic; second, that students only learn when they are compelled to do so by positive and negative sanctions; and third, that a good job is only attainable with a degree. As these myths break down, administrators are finding their jobs impossible, for all concerned are demanding more freedom.

The university is based on an industrial-era model of turning out "products" rather than on the reality of the communications era we are entering. Changes must therefore be based on a new understanding of education — or perhaps more accurately on a revival of an old understanding: Education must prepare the individual to develop himself to the full in the environment which exists and will exist during his life time. Given the fact that we will be engaged primarily in moving information in coming decades, it is accurate to state that life must be seen as learning rather than earning.

The purpose of the school must be to *learn to learn*. The process of learning to learn, however, inevitably involves participation rather than passive reception; learning to learn involves doing rather than sitting. The teacher in this form of education is one who knows how to teach a "style" rather than facts; age or experience is not the key to being a good teacher. It is for this reason that nine- and ten-year-olds are often the best teachers of seven- and eight-year-olds.

The rapidly rising costs of both public and private universities threaten their future; it is necessary to pay high salaries to teachers and administrators and to provide food, clothing and shelter as they "prepare" to contribute to life. Universities can greatly reduce their costs and increase their contributions to society as they recognize: first, that students do learn by doing — for example, the most efficient method of learning about the problem of poverty may be to be active in securing its elimination; second, that people learn when knowledge is related to problem/possibilities in which they are interested, rather than around disciplines; and third, that the best teachers may well be those actively involved with the problem/possibilities, rather than with the theoretical and academic.

In effect, if universities and colleges are to survive they must move in one of two directions — or indeed in both simultaneously. Either they must become the "communications and information center" of the community in which they are located, or they must become the center of knowledge about a specific problem/possibility of state, national or international interest. The universities which continue to turn out graduates equipped only with theoretical knowledge of disciplines are fated to die.

The universities afford one of the major opportunities for growth and change. Both students and professors demand the opportunity for participation. Once it is perceived that action, for example, in a poverty program results in true learning we will be able to reduce the costs of learning and thus reduce the pressure on state budgets and parents' pockets. It is neither natural nor necessary that students be cut off from real life while in the university. Their learning can often be paid for as they engage in tasks which are significant for them and for the society. Nor is it essential that most teachers earn all their living expenses from teaching. Many teachers in coming years will work at their chosen professions and supplement their income by teaching part-time. Evidence shows that alive students may be the best way to challenge obsolete — but still accepted — shibboleths in the professions; thus real teaching may be the best way to keep one's knowledge growing.

Third, and most surprisingly perhaps, you could become involved in the creation of new forms of publication. I believe it is clear that existing newspapers, magazines, etc. no longer respond to the real needs of readers, nor do they take advantage of the new techniques of printing. Readers today seek depth but are being given superficial statements about immediate events.

For example, one might create a new monthly publication which tackled a different specific problem/possibility each month. (An initial attempt at this format has already been developed in book form by the Bobbs-Merrill *Dialogue* Series,[2] but it needs to be translated into magazine format if it is to be truly successful.) Each issue would contain three parts: first, a dialogue focuser which would set out in brief form the agreements on a particular topic, the disagreements about the topic, and the areas out of which new agreements might emerge; second, a number of articles setting out the different views presently held about the problem/possibilities; and third, a "psyche bank" which sets out the present fragmented ideas which apparently hold the key to the resolution of the present disagreements. (It is assumed, in effect, that the way to resolve a disagreement — or paradox — is to raise it to the next higher level of argument where the paradox vanishes.) This form of presentation can be adapted to both video and audio media.

Let me list briefly some other steps which need to be taken: Public and private bureaucracies must move from seeing themselves as mechanisms for control of the public to seeing themselves as organisms designed to serve the developing needs of the public. State and national legislatures and executives must provide the public with wider and wider familiarity with their operations. All organizations must learn how to re-structure themselves to facilitate internal communi-cation rather than to ensure internal control. This point is continuously made by management con-sultants, although they do not yet seem to know how to translate their prescriptions into models.

I am sure my basic thesis that the Pacific Northwest can lead in these areas remains absurdly optimistic for many of you. Let me therefore reemphasize my initial point. Our only real hope is that the areas outside the Northeast — the South, the Southwest, the Northwest, the Plains States and Appalachia — will realize their potentials and challenge the out-moded values of the industrial age which are still being defended by the Northeast.

[1] Some 200 groups of Chicagoans participated in a two-part televised program on the city's educational crisis. The second part of the series incorporated feedback from group activity sparked by the initial presentation.

[2] See Working Appendix on *Dialogue* Series.

This chapter was adapted from a speech originally given to the

Governors' Conference on Perspectives for the Future, Seattle,
Washington, June 22, 1969.

This chapter is excerpted from the introductory "Dialogue-Focuser: Women," in *Dialogue on Women,* one of a series of *Dialogue* books under the general editorship of Robert Theobald (see Working Appendix for further information on the series). Its inclusion here serves several purposes: it deals with one of the powerless groups in our society, it provides additional insight into some of the generalizations made in "Glimpses of an Alternative Future," it provides further clarification of the alternative views of man explicated throughout this volume and it partially illustrates the "dialogue" approach to the formulation and statement of issues in controversy about which Theobald often talks.

A Dialogue-Focuser is a different style of document. Its purpose is to summarize briefly the state of the debate on a particular subject.

Like the Dialogue-Focusers in other volumes of its series, its authorship is the product of an extended dialogue and only incidentally that of the man who put it on paper.

Editors

AGREEMENT

The role which women have played, their own self-image and the image that men have had of them have varied widely from culture to culture and from one historical period to another. There has, however, been one factor common to all cultures and time periods — that babies were born to women as a result of sexual activity. This common factor has limited the range of variation in cultural patterns although it must be recognized that the limits have still been extraordinarily wide. Values which are considered essentially masculine in one culture are considered feminine in others; roles which are played only by men in certain areas of the world are played only by women in others.

The necessary linking of sexual activity to procreation is already essentially broken and with it the physiological basis for the double standard of sex which demanded purity in women but accepted premarital sexual activity for men. The range of contraceptive devices is now so wide that it is possible to ensure, with almost complete certainty, that unwanted conceptions do not occur. Projected developments, such as a birth control capsule which will release its ingredients over an extended period of time, will effectively eliminate the remaining risk.

In addition, there is evidence that the taboos about abortion, as well as birth control, are dropping. There is growing agreement that the healthy emotional development of a child depends on those around him being willing to provide the love he requires if he is to develop into a sane, healthy individual. The combination of these developments means that it is possible for sexual activity to be almost completely divorced from procreation.

Two other factors in this general area are also generally agreed. First, it is clear that the degree of population pressure throughout the world, and particularly in the poor countries, is now such that the average size of families must be reduced if overcrowding and famine are to be avoided. Second, it is not only possible to avoid conception when it is not desired, it is also increasingly possible to ensure conception for all those who desire it. The number of women who want to bear children but are denied this possibility has already declined abruptly and will continue to decline.

It is perhaps less clearly recognized that the linkage between procreation and sexual activity is being shattered in the opposite sense also: procreation is increasingly possible without sexual activity. The first limited steps were taken in this direction with the acceptance of artificial insemination for those unable to have babies through sexual relations with their husbands. Some people are now calling for the extension of this possibility to mothers who would prefer that their children partook of the hereditary characteristics of some man whom they admired: it has been suggested that a sperm bank should be created for this purpose. Others have argued for clonal reproduction: the creation of an exact replica of a human person presently alive. Still others are working to create life in a test tube. There are few, if any, who are prepared to state confidently that none of these techniques can be achieved.

Finally, it is far from certain that sexual pleasure must necessarily be related to human sexual relationships: it might well be possible to create more "efficient" sex pleasure through the use of electrical or mechanical machines rather than through human sexual activity.

The new debate about women and the relationships between men and women therefore centers around which of these potentially possible physiological developments are desirable and what social attitudes will facilitate, hinder or prevent them. It is clear, of course, that full acceptance of some of these techniques would make it possible, and necessary, to create female-male relationships totally anew.

DISAGREEMENT

One side of the debate claims that present definitions of masculinity — and femininity which has been largely defined in reference to it — force man's and woman's nature into a cultural straight-jacket, and the values presently accepted are dangerous to the survival of the world. They argue that the dominant masculine values — strength, vigor, competitiveness, power — do not fit the new conditions apparently emerging.

It is argued that the main purpose of the new society must be to permit the development of each individual to his maximum potential and to provide him with a social environment in which this can be achieved. Two key views about the nature of the good society are advanced: first, the necessity of diversity, of a wide range of personalities and attitudes through providing each individual with the circumstances in which he can discover who he is; second, life cannot consist in the setting of specific goals which must be achieved, but rather must be oriented toward process.

Effective opposition to this view hardly exists. This is not because the view is accepted but rather because it appears so irrelevant to the present leaders of governmental, administrative and voluntary organizations who generally see the appropriate goals in terms of a higher gross national product, more goods and services and greater control over the environment. Man's needs are seen as unlimited and the basic goal of the society must be to satisfy these needs. It is therefore argued in much of the literature that the failure of women to emerge as equal partners with men is due to the fact that they have not adopted the characteristics which can be clearly seen as crucial for success in the present socioeconomic system, and that women should therefore concentrate on developing these values and "strengths."

Disagreement with this latter view does not challenge the statement that women have been relatively unsuccessful within the present culture. Nor does it deny that women could change and be more successful. Rather it is argued that the areas presently valued will not be important in the future and that it is therefore absurd to abandon female values at this point. It is suggested that the major areas of work in coming periods will be education, the human care of human beings and the creation of the good community, and that these will demand empathy, intuition and cooperation which appear to be predominantly female characteristics.

This theme has been developed further by certain

women's groups, such as Women's Strike for Peace, who have argued that feminine values are crucial to the controlling and development of the world even today. They claim that women have the capacity to do certain presently crucial tasks better than men. Believing that force is counterproductive on the national and international scene, they state that women must now take the initiative because men have been taught to try to achieve "power" in all situations.

power	cooperation
competitiveness	empathy
strength	process
force	intuition

This view is countered on two levels. First, it is argued that the only way to bring about change is to force through a new idea or a new technique — that cooperation cannot be effective in changing the behavior of people. Second, it is argued that it is impossible to change people, that the world will always be ordered by force and that it is, therefore, naive to look for alternative techniques which would eliminate force. At the next level of analysis, these two arguments appear identical: it is claimed that competition is necessary and will prevail over cooperation.

Perhaps the most rapidly growing debate is around the desirable nature of the family — and by extension the community with whom the family or the individual has close relationships. Examination of this issue stems from a belief that we are now in the process of moving from the industrial age into a cybernated era and that this involves changing the basis of our society from a production-transportation net to an information net.

The effective functioning of an information net, however, would require fundamental shifts in the attitudes of the society; for information can only be moved effectively in an honest, cooperative society. This statement is based on the now clearly proven fact that power and distortion of information are linked: the individual in a subordinate position passes information up the line which he believes his superiors would like to hear. The acceptance of an information net as the basis of society would therefore inherently require greater acceptance of what might be defined as female characteristics.

If the culture will, in fact, be based on an information net rather than a production-transportation net, it will be possible to reduce substantially the degree of mobility. People could then determine for themselves, without outside constraints, how often they would like to move, how much children would like to see of their parents at what points in their lives, how much parents would like to see their children at what points in their lives and how the possible conflicts could be resolved.

While a debate on this topic is just beginning, it is important to note that there are many attempts to work out these issues through living them. The present lifestyles and thinking range all the way from the preservation of the nuclear family to the creation of new forms of community groups, from intense personalism to institutionalization.

This debate also appears irrelevant to many. It is argued in rebuttal that we are living in the high period of the industrial culture, that man has learned to produce what is needed for a decent standard of living and that we have developed both the tools and the institutions to ensure that this standard will be shared by all. According to this view the basic lines of human advance for the future are still those which have been laid down in the past: there are no new factors in the environment which make it necessary for the culture to adapt fundamentally.

If this view is correct, the debate about the appropriate family structure is indeed essentially irrelevant, for the structures of the industrial age essentially foreclose debate on this topic. Overwhelming pressures force an ever-growing proportion of workers to move; this has meant that families have generally been reduced to the nuclear level, thus containing mother, father and minor children.

Arguments about the structuring of families and communities are cross-cut by a debate about freedom, permanency and commitment. Some believe that the whole idea of the family as a permanent bond is a cultural hang-over which should be eliminated. It is argued that it is essential that each individual be free to grow away from another as well as to grow toward him, that no substantial number of human relationships would be permanent if they were not supported, and indeed demanded, by social pressures. Individuals should, therefore, have the right to relate to one another for as long as seems good to them and there should be no expectation of permanency.

This approach is countered by the argument that permanency can only be created through commitment, that it is permanency which permits finding oneself in another and thus finding one's own self. Willingness to try to help another is essential to one's growth in this view; getting to know a person well enough takes a lifetime.

All the previous issues are cross-cut by yet another: the argument as to whether we will be able to improve the genetic inheritance, the emotional behavior, the intelligence of the human being through the use of human engineering. It is argued that the only possible way to improve the human race rapidly enough to face the present crises is to use all of our scientific knowledge to achieve this end. Manipulation of the genetic structure first, followed by the actual creation of life, are essential, it is claimed.

It appears that this stance must necessarily be based on the belief that fundamental shifts in bodily functions can occur without any major unfavorable effects on the organism in either the short-or the long-run — that we have the power to engineer our own bodies. In this view, the physiological differences between men and women can also be expected to yield to the culture; there is an effective possibility of producing any cultural pattern which seems desirable. Such a position means that there are no effective constraints in remaking the human race: man can choose to structure his body and his culture in any way which seems good to him.

Disagreement with this approach occurs at two levels. First, it is claimed that it may be reasonably expected that there are rather severe limits to the ability of any organism — including our own bodies — to adapt and that it is extraordinarily difficult to predict the effects of any change. This argument is based on a statement in theoretical cybernetics (the science of communication and control) that any change in a system will bring about further changes both expected and unexpected. It is also based on practical observations of the consequences of relatively minor bodily changes, such as the slight — but continuing — increase in body height. Most of those who adopt this view also appear to argue that there are substantial physiological differences between the sexes and that cultural standardization cannot submerge these differences without the potential for highly unfavorable consequences.

The second level of challenge is philosophical and

metaphysical. It results from belief that the important quality of a human being or social system — that of completeness or holism — does not lend itself to improvement through objective analysis alone. It is, in a very real sense, on a different dimension. It involves the acceptance of mystery, of the ultimate inability to know everything. This acceptance of unknowability may derive from many sources — from religion or ethics or science — but it always leads away from an acceptance of "objective" manipulation.

In this view the problem of mankind cannot be solved by improving any one dimension of his being, such as his speed or his intelligence. Rather it is mankind's ability to define his own private self in relationship to a small number of other beings which determines the meaning of human life. Improvement in this dimension will be achieved by learning how to communicate genuinely — an ability which seems to have been largely destroyed during the industrial age. Progress in this direction does not depend primarily on "improved" physical or mental characteristics but rather on commitment to achieve communication.

In effect, this final argument is about the proper relation of ends and means. One group argues that improvements in the minds and bodies of human beings would lead to improvements in the quality of human life. The other group argues that we should aim to improve the quality of human life and that physical and mental improvement would result. It is this disagreement which leads the first group to call the second naive and vague, and the second to call the first instrumental and manipulative; it is this disagreement which is perhaps most in need of resolution and yet most difficult to resolve.

The name of Robert Theobald has for many become synonymous with the concept of the Guaranteed Income. It would
be impossible, therefore, to produce a volume of his writings
and speeches without including materials on this subject. The
reader should be aware, however, that Mr. Theobald has gone
far beyond the guaranteed income in his thinking about social
change. When he published *Free Men and Free Markets* in
1962, he assumed that the introduction of Basic Economic
Security and Committed Spending would bring about the
change in social and psychological attitudes essential for a
more humanistic society. He has since come to realize that a
change in social and psychological attitudes is essential to the
recognition of the guaranteed income as a necessity. It is this
latter realization which explains his present concern with
numerous issues not specifically economic.

The fully developed rationale for the guaranteed income can
be found in three books, *Free Men and Free Markets* by
Robert Theobald, *The Guaranteed Income* edited by Robert
Theobald, and *Committed Spending* edited by Robert
Theobald. Readers who are inclined to reject the concept on
the basis of unanswered questions and objections raised by our
selections, or to accept the concept uncritically, are urged to
read these books before rendering their final judgment.

It is ironic that one nation in the world is nearing economic
abundance, while at the same time most countries of the world
are yet to enjoy the luxury of running water. However, this is
a fact. In the near future the onslaught of cybernation and
technology may actually make a job a scarce commodity. The
man who is employed in the future may be as rare as the man
who is unemployed today. The reader may laugh at this statement, but Mr. Theobald feels certain that such a situation is
developing faster than most of us realize. This constitutes one
of the major reasons why he feels that every American must be
given the right to a guaranteed income, so as to live with
security in the future years.

Our economic system is bringing abundance to our doorstep far sooner than we believed possible, and has done its job so well that we will undoubtedly see the system become obsolete in the near future. In short, our economic system is working its way out of a job. The guaranteed income suggests the type of economic system which is a must if every American is to live with dignity and security in the coming years.

Editors

REVOLUTION IN ATTITUDE

A revolution in our view of income distribution occurred in the 1960's. When the decade started, poverty was perceived generally as a marginal phenomenon which was vanishing rapidly as wealth expanded in the United States. By the end of the decade we were aware that hunger and poverty were severe problems and that only a massive societal effort would ensure their eradication.

How have we reached this point? I think that we must credit four different factors. First, there was the effect of the pioneering analysts at the end of the fifties and in the early sixties. Michael Harrington's book *The Other America* was most commented upon but it was only one work among others. As the decade advanced it became impossible to ignore the evidence which showed that despite massive increases in wealth and low levels of unemployment, hunger and poverty persisted in the United States and indeed deepened in many areas.

Second, the theme of a guaranteed income emerged

from two apparently divergent philosophic traditions in the early sixties (it now seems that the divergence was more apparent than real). The theme of the guaranteed income is really very simple: the best way to abolish poverty is to provide income as a matter of right to all those who are poor. One argument for this approach was put forward by Milton Friedman in his volume *Capitalism and Freedom,* and the other in my own volume *Free Men and Free Markets.* The considerable amount of literature since published, including my *The Guaranteed Income,* has forced public attention upon the statistics of poverty and the reasons for it. Later in the decade other proposals for profound reform of the present welfare system — such as family allowances and a national welfare system — emerged and gained national attention. These proposals and the guaranteed income proposals have become staples of government reports and public debate to such an extent that the Gallup poll has been taking periodic surveys on the attitudes of the public to the guaranteed income issue. A federal commission was appointed to prepare a report on the issue of income maintenance. And in August 1969 President Nixon announced a welfare reform plan which included guaranteed annual income provisions.

Third, a national movement developed among welfare recipients in the mid-sixties which aimed to force welfare departments not only to provide all people with the payments they were due under the law but also hoped to widen the types of payments which were available. This movement has had considerable local effect and some national impact; it has often been able to dramatize its cause when local and national authorities have tried to restrict even present limited benefits.

Fourth, the mayors of many cities and the governors of many states have been driven to recognize that unless welfare burdens can in some way be lessened they will be unable to find funds for all essential needs. This profound and immediate reality has pushed the poverty and hunger issue into the center of the political arena for the first time. The decision of Governor Rockefeller to demand national welfare legislation and the reaction to Senator McGovern's committee's work on hunger make it clear that the issue will come to the fore within the term of the present administration.

I am not suggesting that politicians are happy with this situation. They know that there is little honor and kudos to be gained here. But the hunger issue is now on the agenda along with two other key domestic issues, youth and crime, and steps must be taken to deal with all three of them. The combination of the steps which we take in these three areas will determine whether we take advantage of the freedom promised by the new technologies or whether we move into a police state.

WAR ON POVERTY

What then are the alternatives? We must start with the potential of the war on poverty. This program has failed; it is only a question of how soon we will understand the reality of this failure.

Being poor consists of a lack of money

To be poor is to have too little money. The immediate need of the poor is for more money. The immediate need is not moral uplift, cultural refinements, extended education, retraining programs or makework jobs, but more money.

This is the belief of the advocates of the guaranteed income. This view is much too simple for the sophisticated defenders of the status quo, who argue that we must provide the poor with the skills which would enable them to earn an adequate wage and who ignore the fact that the majority of the poor cannot or should not hold jobs which would allow them to earn a decent wage.

The barriers to the elimination of poverty are not economic: the funds which will be released at the end of the Vietnam war would suffice to allow the introduction of the guaranteed income. The barriers are moral and social. The United States is not willing to apply its vast productive potential to the elimination of poverty and hides its unwillingness with statements about the need for motivation and incentives.

Supporters of the guaranteed income and supporters of the poverty program not only propose different programs but have different ends in view. The supporters of the poverty program see man as an inefficient machine to be reprogrammed from time to time as machines make his existing skills obsolete. The destruction of his work and life pattern is regretted but seen as unavoidable. Indeed, one can go further and argue that the generally accepted goals of our society appear to be technological wizardry, economic efficiency and the developed individual in the good society, but in that order. I often fear that we persist in this order of priorities because we no longer want to know more about human beings and human systems of organization. Compared to a (necessarily) functionally neat, clean, odorless, efficient and continuously functioning cybernetic machine system, a unit of mankind is messy, smelly, disobedient, quarrelsome, lazy and a walking source of error. For those already in a state of emotional and sensory atrophy, a machine is easier to get on with than a man.

It is the essentially dehumanized approach of the poverty program which ensures that it cannot be successful. I am, of course, aware that there are many people within the poverty program who attempt to use its potential to benefit individuals, but they are fighting the basic thrust of the whole program and their efforts will always be insignificant compared to the total size of the problem. The goal of the poverty program is not to help people to find themselves but rather to push them back into the industrial system just as fast and as often as they are forced out of it.

The failures of the poverty program are being increasingly recognized, but there is still insufficient understanding of the fact that the failure of the poverty program was inevitable from the day of its creation. It is critically important that we realize that the program did not fail because of bad luck or bad administration: it failed because it was poorly conceived. This is now a commonplace statement and it may appear like second-guessing after the fact. In order to demonstrate that it was possible to tell that failure was inevitable before the program even began, I quote at length from a speech which I gave immediately after the program was announced:

"Let me make it perfectly clear that I do not impugn the motivations of those who are developing the President's poverty program: I am simply convinced that they have so far failed to understand the true nature of poverty in a cybernated era, an era where the computer is combined with advanced machinery. The present program assumes that poverty can be eliminated through Federal action. I, on the other hand, believe that poverty can only be abolished by motivating the individual and the community. I am against the simplistic laws coined by Parkinson; however, for those who appreciate them, may I suggest one of my own — that the number of helpless poor inevitably increases with the number of bureaucrats trying to aid them.

"I believe that the President's poverty program as presently drawn is unsatisfactory. Let me list several reasons: First, as I have already stated, the present bill is based, both in letter and spirit, on an over-emphasis on only one direction in what should be essentially a two-directional process: on the central government telling the state and the locality what to do. I believe that such an approach will necessarily fail. Second, the proposal to aid small farmers and small businessmen through small-scale financial aid has no chance of success in the light of the realities of the cybernated era — it is now impossible to turn a small, struggling farmer into a small, successful farmer or a small, struggling businessman into a small, successful businessman, merely through the provision of very limited sums of money. Third, the proposed types of training camps, clearly modelled on the experience of the CCC of the thirties, are no longer appropriate for the social and economic conditions of the sixties. In the industrial age, which still existed in the thirties, if you put a person in a camp and kept him there for six months or a year you were able in many cases to provide him with the limited skills and education required to make him an effective member of society. This technique will not work in a cyber-nated era, for the education and skills required to become a functioning member of society are not now teachable in this way.

"The consequences of setting up such camps will, in these circumstances, be unsatisfactory and possibly dangerous; for while adults still have not understood the realities of this age, our children are fully aware. Let me give you an example: a Mexican gang in Los Angeles was being helped by an assistant to a Congressman. This assistant asked one of the members of the gang: "What are you going to do when you grow up?" One child said: "I'm going to college," but the others promptly shut him up with the argument: "Don't kid him along. He's a good Joe. You know you're not going to college." And this is what is radically new about our situation. Up until now, the vast majority of the poor in America have never really felt poor, for they believed that they were going to be all right — or if they had given up hope for themselves, they were convinced that their children were going to be all right. Today, we have a poor class who know they are poor and who know they are going to stay poor.

"Finally, passage of the existing program will destroy the urgency which is increasingly felt — it will make it appear as though we have a program although we actually do not. The amount of money proposed, as has often been pointed out, is not even enough to finance a skirmish against poverty. The war on poverty must be placed in the proper context if we are to win it. At the outset we must recognize that the cost of the campaign on poverty is not the problem — that we can easily afford to provide the required funds. The first step is to recognize that the problem is not economic but moral, psychological and social — how do we challenge the individual and the community so that they will strive to overcome their problems? The second step to winning the war on poverty is to recognize that full employment is an obsolete goal — that the drive to provide toil is obsolete and that the true challenge is to educate people in such a way that they can live a life which will appear meaningful to them, and to their fellowmen.

**the cybernated era based on full education
means the end of the industrial age
based on full employment**

"We must comprehend that the emergence of the cybernated era based on full education means the end of the industrial age based on full employment. This means that the parts of the country which have not yet been brought into the industrial system cannot possibly pass through the industrialization process. This will appear disastrous to many whose highest goal is to enter the industrial age — I, on the contrary, consider it most fortunate. The industrial age required that everybody toil — the cybernated era will allow everybody a reasonable standard of living without toil and will allow the development of a better society.

"It is now becoming clear that the values of the

industrial age were deeply destructive of human and community values and that it will be extraordinarily difficult for the industrial parts of the country and the world to create the values necessary to a satisfactory life in the non-toil, non-consumption oriented cybernated era.

"Our key problem stems from the fact that we have made the value of a man synonymous with the economic value of the toil he performs: we fail to recognize that people should have a claim on resources even if they do not toil. The measure of destruction of our values is, I believe, shown in the fact that those living in an industrial society find it natural that people do not receive an adequate amount of food, clothing and shelter even though there is surplus food in storage and the possibility of producing more housing and more clothing if we gave people the money to buy them. We can contrast this view with that of the so-called primitive societies; in many of these it was literally impossible to starve unless the whole community was starving. George Peter Murdoch, the celebrated anthropologist, described the reaction of one group of natives when he tried to explain the problem of the poor in Western countries. There was stark disbelief: 'How can he have no food? Does he have no friends? How can he have no house? Does he have no neighbors?'

"The poverty in the Western world can only be explained by a failure of conscience, by an unfounded and heartless belief that the poor have only themselves to blame for their situation. The minimum step which we must take if we are to eliminate the poverty which exists in the United States is to introduce the guaranteed income.''

I see no reason to change significantly any portion of these analyses. We must therefore return to first principles and examine what route is available to deal significantly with the problems of hunger and poverty.

GUARANTEED EMPLOYMENT VS GUARANTEED INCOME

The first route which might be suggested, but which I would hope that we would exclude from serious consideration, is that of putting the reality of hunger and poverty back out of consciousness. I hope that the genie is out and that the society would no longer tolerate our putting it back into the bottle. Society must now choose between two primary directions, both of which have fundamental implications but which move in diametrically opposed directions. We can try to ensure that everybody is able to find a job and therefore is able to earn an income, or we can set up a system in which every individual receives an income as a matter of right and is given the responsibility to develop himself and his society.

A recent Gallup poll makes it abundantly clear that the American people prefer the first alternative; that is, a very substantial number of people prefer the idea of guaranteed employment to the idea of guaranteed income. In fact, however, this choice would actually destroy the social and economic patterns of behavior which America most values.

Guaranteed employment represents a continuation of past traditions. It claims that human beings should hold a job if they are to be entitled to an income. Implicit in this proposal is a conviction of the dignity of work, the requirement that each individual contribute to the society, the unwillingness to provide resources to those who are merely parasitic on the society. It is not surprising that Americans, when they come to understand the reality of hunger and poverty, should opt for this approach.

Unfortunately, the guaranteed employment proposal is based, like the war on poverty, on an understanding of reality which is from the past rather than of the future. In the 1930's, people couldn't find jobs because there was no demand for the products they produced. Most of the unemployed had meaningful skills in terms of the technology of the period and could be absorbed as demand increased, a fact shown by the way unemployment melted as war needs increased. Today, however, there is no lack of demand in the overall job market for those with meaningful skills. It is those who have inadequate training, inadequate skills or problems such as bad health, alcoholism, etc., who cannot find jobs today.

Training programs, in so far as they are successful, remove people from the unemployable class. The proposal for government as the employer of last resort recognizes implicitly that not everybody can be retrained to be useful in the conventional job market, and that only specially created job opportunities will absorb such people.

But what activities are those unemployable in the normal job market going to be able to do? If they are unemployable in the normal job market, where will there be meaningful activity for them? Few activities today can be based on an unskilled, uneducated or unreliable work force, and yet this is what the government will have to provide as employer of last resort.

We must recognize the reality of the problem: there are a growing number of people who are not competitive with machines today. To take one example, it is not economical to employ people to dig ditches in competition with a ditch-digging machine. Even leaf raking requires intelligence and responsibility unless it is *pure* make-work.

What, then, of the dynamics of any program designed to ensure that anybody who cannot find an income through a conventional job should be able to go to the government in its capacity as employer of last resort? The government must inevitably find itself confronted with the most ill-trained, ill-educated, disinterested part of the population. The activity into which these people would have to be moved would always be boring and usually be meaningless. Those who wished to work meaningfully would rebel against the meaninglessness and the trouble would be encouraged by those who had been forced into the program against their will. Absenteeism would be high and work standards abysmally low, while heavy demands for changes in activity would endanger the efficiency of the program.

Congress would find the situation intolerable. It would be argued that advantage was being taken of the program, that administrative lines were ineffi- cient. Assuming that the program continued, there would be pressure to tighten up and to introduce rules to prevent abuse. One might imagine proposals, for example, that nobody should be permitted to change his job more than once every six months and that those who had a consistent record of absen- teeism should be fined part of their wage if they failed to turn up for their work.

This scenario for the future is shared by others, although it is not accepted by most economists. Al- most all science fiction writers — the best futurists in our society — who have examined this issue have con- cluded that such an evolution is inevitable if we continue to develop technology and yet demand that everybody should hold a job. The science fiction novel most to this point is *Player Piano* by Kurt Vonnegut.

What then of the basic goals of those who propose "guaranteed employment?" Will they be fulfilled? We have seen that the work people carry out in this program will not add to their dignity, for it will be make-work which can better be carried out by machines. We have seen that these people will not contribute to society, for if they had the skills to do so — or could be trained to have the skills to do so — they would not need to apply to the government as an employer of last resort.

Finally, the attempt to keep these people in jobs would actually decrease the wealth available to the society rather than increase it. The scarcest commodity in this society is organizational skills. Running this program would be extremely difficult and would require very high levels of skills which would have to be diverted from other valuable uses while the production achieved by the employed labor force would not be significant. Thus the decision to employ the unemployables would actually decrease wealth.

Should we then abandon the goals of achieving dignity from work and requiring that each individual contribute to the society? Of course not. Man is a striving animal and the destruction of the opportunity for achieving meaning will inevitably destroy him. In addition, it is clear that the survival of any social system requires that all its members work toward the survival and development of the society. We do not need to abandon our fundamental goals; rather, we need to discover how they can be effectively fulfilled in present circumstances.

We do, however, need to make a distinction between our fundamental goals and those which have come to be seen as immediately necessary. We have developed a society in which efficiency and maximum consumption have become critical both to many individuals and to the functioning of society. If we are to consider the issues involved in the distribution of income we have to accept that the most important requirement is that each individual should be given the maximum opportunity for self-development in a social structure in which he can function effectively.

This approach is, in reality, the main point of disagreement between those who perceive the necessity for man to be employed and those who believe that man should be set free by being provided with his income as a right and by being encouraged to accept the responsibility for developing himself and his society. Those in favor of jobs accept a view of man which is derived from the work of Professor B. F. Skinner, who argues that men respond only to positive and negative sanctions — the carrot and the whip. They argue that if human beings are not afraid of losing their jobs and not enthusiastic about achieving higher standards of living they will sink back into apathy — or, in more colorful language, they will sit in front of the television set all day swilling beer.

A new school of psychologists has emerged to challenge the assumptions of Skinner and to argue that man is capable of self-development. Perhaps the most developed theoretical scheme stems from the work of Abraham Maslow, who argues that man's patterns of behavior change as his situation changes. So long as man does not possess the food, clothing and shelter he needs for survival he places his energy into creating the material necessities for life. But as soon as man moves beyond the necessity to strive for material goods he is driven by his own internal necessities to try to discover what will allow him to develop his own capabilities.

If Maslow is right, as I believe he is, his theory demonstrates the profound immorality of the present welfare system and all techniques which use the whip and the carrot. Individuals who are provided with insufficient money to feed, clothe and shelter themselves adequately are simply incapable of rising above their immediate material needs to consider the wider possibilities that face them. In the words of a welfare recipient, "If you're hungry it's very hard to think beyond where and when the next meal will come from."

If Skinner is right, the whip and carrot technique is necessary. While we may deplore it we dare not modify it for fear that the society will break down as more and more people fail to contribute to the necessities of the society. If, on the other hand, Maslow is right, the present welfare system is the very pattern which is preventing large numbers of individuals from contributing as they could to the development of the society.

One's view of the proper pattern for the future therefore depends on one's view of human nature. Such views cannot be proven correct on the basis of objective data, for the way that people behave depends very much on the attitudes toward them of the society and of the individual observing them. If the society treats a group of individuals as though they are lazy, irresponsible bums, it sets up patterns so that the only "sane" form of behavior is to *be* a lazy, irresponsible bum. This is like the case of the paranoid who, believing that all other people are threatening, acts in such a way that the reaction of others becomes threatening to him. If Maslow is right then the younger generation which has grown up in an abundance economy are looking for ways in which they can engage in self-development. Unfortunately, however, there are few routes by which they can contribute to the society. In their frustration, therefore, they are led to draw attention to their needs through protest, which sometimes becomes violent.

Individuals treated *as* lazy *become* lazy

I consider such violence unwise, but I consider the attempts to suppress and drive it underground even more dangerous. The young people in our society are warning us by their actions that there are serious problems and that we must pay attention to them. If we should continue our present pattern of repression we may succeed in "calming" the country, but we will do so at the cost of suppressing those very symptoms which might lead the country to re-examine itself. We will do it also at the cost of breaking the heart of the very generation which must save us, by instead driving them to drugs, drink, sexual excess and meaningless crime.

The unwisdom of our present patterns of activity can be seen most clearly if we consider a physical analogy. The body runs a high temperature in many diseases and this serves as a symptom to alert the doctor to the need for action. He would be considered stupid if he acted simply to reduce the temperature without consideration to the causes of the temperature. Similarly we show no intelligence if we try to reduce the temperature of the body politic without considering the reasons for that temperature.

Now let us turn to the method of introduction of the guaranteed income. I have become convinced that the means proposed in my 1963 book, *Free Men and Free Markets*, are no longer desirable. This book stated that we should provide additional resources to every individual if his income should fall below a certain level, but that we should recognize the need for a premium to those who worked at jobs seen as desirable by the society. Even at the time of writing *Free Men and Free Markets* I stated that this premium was largely necessary because of the present views of the society rather than in terms of the ethical or economic requirements of the situation. It now seems clear to me that we must eliminate the idea that income rights should be different if the individual holds a job or not.

There are two reasons for this. First, negative income tax schemes, based upon payment of the difference between a given income level set by the government and the individual's present (lower) income raise incredibly complex problems of calculation. They also provide major possibilities for cheating and it would be naive to assume that some cheating will not take place. Such schemes would also tend to encourage new patterns of disintegration in family life.

Guaranteed income should be administered in the following way. Every individual in the United States should receive a direct payment from the federal government, which would not be affected by his present income. The level of this income would have to be set in the light of fiscal possibilities and the commitment of the American people to provide resources. The goal, however, should be $1,400 per adult and $900 per child.

All other income received from any source would be taxed. The individual exemptions and almost all tax deductions would be eliminated. The amount of tax paid would depend only on the amount of money received by the individual rather than the source of the income. The degree of progression in the tax rate and the overall pattern of income distribution would depend on the views of the public about the degree of inequality it felt was appropriate and justified.

COMMITTED SPENDING

In this context, I am convinced that we must be prepared not only to provide resources to those who are poor but also to deal with the other acute problem of income distribution — the problems which will confront those now in middle-income groups who will see their earning opportunities destroyed as the computer continues to develop. That is, not only will there be an increasingly inadequate number of market-supported jobs for those with lower levels of education and skills, but it can also be expected that many of those now engaged in middle management and similar occupations will lose their present jobs and be felt by prospective employers to have insufficient intellectual flexibility to take on new types of work. The drastic and abrupt drop in income which will follow will mean that members of this group will find themselves suddenly unable to meet the expenditure commitments already undertaken as part of their way of life, both on a day-to-day basis and incorporated in their long-term plans. In contemplating the possibility of hardship for the individuals in this group, we should not forget that their personal difficulties will have far wider implications for society as a whole. For just as individuals need the support of some form of basic economic security, society needs support for its standards and a source of initiatives and drive to move it toward its goals. It is this support, these initiatives and this drive which are supplied by this group. As an alternative to allowing the complete disruption of the way of life of this standard-supporting and societally useful group, it is necessary that a method be devised to maintain its level of incomes.

Therefore, in addition to *guaranteed income,* a second principle should be introduced, embodying the concept of the need to protect the existing middle-income group against abrupt major declines in their standard of living; this principle could be called *committed spending.* Together the principles of guaranteed income and committed spending could be called an Economic Security Plan, a plan designed to provide security for society as a whole and for each individual within it.

The payments to those receiving committed spending from the government would be related to their incomes before they became eligible for payments under committed spending. The continuance of higher levels of income for those entitled to committed spending, compared to those available under guaranteed income, would allow the middle-income group to continue the expenditures to which they had become committed and which are vital to the short-run stability of the country. However, to avoid major differentials in entitlements, no payment under committed spending would exceed a given multiple of the amount available to a family of the same size under guaranteed income. This multiple might possibly be three; thus, if a family receiving guaranteed income would be entitled, for example, to $3,700 then a

120

family of comparable size would have an income ceiling of $11,100 from committed spending.

IMPLICATIONS

Now let me return to the basic guaranteed income plan. Having developed some of the reasons why the guaranteed income is the least bad way to deal with the present crisis in welfare, I would like to suggest some of the implications of the adoption of such a policy in terms of the future which it would help to create.

First, we must recognize that the introduction of the guaranteed income would lead to a rise in the incomes and salaries which would have to be paid to those doing what they perceive as unpleasant tasks. If a guaranteed income is available, then it is obvious that people will require a higher level income for doing an unpleasant job than in a situation where the individual's only alternative to holding a job is to go hungry. In this context, therefore, the guaranteed income is a profoundly effective guaranteed wage, and its too rapid introduction could lead to dangerous results in pushing up wages faster than the growth in the economy could absorb.

If we permit a relative rise in the wages which are paid for unpleasant work there will be a tendency for the market itself to come into play, with the invention of machines to assume work which people consider unpleasant. On the other hand, the very availability of the guaranteed income and of an income-maintenance plan for those who lose their jobs because of technical change will create a cadre of people who are willing to do pleasant work without additional payment. This in turn will limit the pressure to invent machines to replace things which people do want to do.

In effect, therefore, the decision to introduce both the guaranteed income and committed spending will permit the market to be allowed far freer play than at present, for it will act to reinforce the wishes of people rather than to cut across them. In effect, much of the effort of the society is presently going toward the invention of equipment to replace attractive rather than unattractive work.

A second result of introducing these two measures will be more far reaching: it will encourage those receiving the guaranteed income and committed spending to join together in consentives to do what they want to do. Consentives will be groups of people with a purpose which binds them together; this purpose can be social or productive. If it is the latter, success in the consentive would lead its members back into the market should this be their wish. The goods produced by these consentives would not compete with mass-produced products available from cybernated productive organizations; the consentive would produce the "custom-designed" goods and services which have been vanishing within the present economy.

122

This type of productive unit would continue far into the future, for the use of a man's hands is one of the most satisfying ways of spending time. The proportion of the population spending most of their time in this kind of production would decline, nevertheless, as other activities seem more challenging and education in its fullest sense takes an ever more central position.

The Protestant work ethic is now obsolete

It is essential that we recognize, however, that we face an acute transitional problem. We can reasonably hope to change the educational process so that those still within it come to recognize that structured toil is unnecessary and to accept the freedom made possible by cybernation. On the other hand, it will be far more difficult to help those brought up within a Protestant work ethic to realize its irrelevance. During the period of transition, will it be necessary to develop political policies to preserve jobs for the older members of society while challenging the young to work in non-structured situations? And if this is indeed necessary, what social mechanisms can we develop to prevent a profound generational split?

The introduction of the guaranteed income would

certainly lessen the incentive to carry out tasks which seem meaningless to the individual involved. It would also increase incentives which would cause the individual to develop himself and his society. This point was well made by Erich Fromm in my book, *The Guaranteed Income.*

Aside from the fact that there is already no work for an ever-increasing sector of the population, and hence that the question of incentive for these people is irrelevant, the question of whether a guaranteed income would not reduce the incentive for work is nevertheless a serious one. I believe, however, that it can be demonstrated that material incentive is by no means the only incentive for work and effort. First of all there are other incentives: pride, social recognition, pleasure in work itself, etc. . . .

"Secondly, it is a fact that man, by nature, is not lazy, but on the contrary, suffers from the results of inactivity. People might prefer not to work for one or two months, but the vast majority would beg to work, even if they were not paid for it. . . .

"Economic abundance, liberation from fear of starvation, would mark the transition from a prehuman to a truly human society."

Both of these developments — new pleasant-unpleasant work patterns and emergence of consentives — imply a long-run development which is critical and far from understood. The guaranteed income makes it possible for people to begin to move outside the artificial scarcity economy in which we are almost all encompassed. In order to live at present, each of us must sell something which is sufficiently scarce that others are willing to buy it. We dare not allow true abundance to emerge for if it should then the prices, wages and salaries which we receive would automatically fall. The greatest rates of gain in income today are therefore received predominantly by those who are most effective in causing artificial scarcity.

Those who move outside this economy of artificial scarcity will begin to produce areas in which goods are free because they are abundant — and also to produce methods of distributing goods which are not dependent on money transfer. As this process develops it will free more people to move outside the "artificial scarcity" economy and it will put downward pressure on prices within the artificial scarcity economy. Thus we can expect to see falling wages, prices and salaries within a relatively short time after the introduction of the guaranteed income and committed spending.

This evolution will be accelerated as we come to understand the necessity for any system to have large amounts of spare capacity to deal with the crises which are inevitable in the operation of any social system. We will learn that we dare not have artificial scarcity because any system which hopes to survive must have built into it the ability to bring massive resources to bear when unusual conditions develop. This means in fact that we must create a society of true abundance and this means in turn that we must move toward a society of free goods and services.

There are two views about our present situation. The dominant one is that we must somehow struggle through with the systems — economic, social, political, legal, etc. — which already exist and that it is totally unrealistic to believe that man can change fundamentally. The view which lies behind intelligent advocacy of the guaranteed income is that in these new conditions which man has himself created he has no option but to grow up, for otherwise he will blow himself up or pollute himself off the face of the earth.

The fundamental issue one faces in examining policies to eliminate poverty is the view of human nature which is built into their proposed implementation. If you believe that we can manipulate individuals into intelligent actions through positive and negative sanctions, then you will be in favor of maintaining a coercive society in which a man will not eat unless he holds a job. In this case you will logically endorse job retraining, the drive for summer jobs however meaningless many of them may be and the idea of government as employer of last resort.

If, on the other hand, you believe that man is inherently a self-striving creature and that he alone can determine his purpose, then you will aim to create a guaranteed income. But you will not stop there. You will try to create the services in all fields — education, skill training, consumer knowledge, child rearing, etc. — which will permit individuals who have been previously underprivileged to realize their potential. We must work with people to provide them with the tools to achieve self development, but we must not demand that they accept *our* goals.

Immediate reaction to these ideas may well be "not politically feasible." I have become somewhat used to this statement, and remember back only a few years when it was said that the mere idea of a guaranteed income was totally unrealistic. Attitudes and events have come a long way during these past few years. Now the President of the United States is talking about some of these ideas. Some fundamental changes in our welfare system have almost certainly become inevitable following the welfare reform plan presented by President Nixon to Congress and to the American people in August 1969. What are some advantages and disadvantages of his proposal?

For one thing, it breaks through one basic barrier to a more intelligent welfare system by admitting that poverty is equally real whether it affects a city dweller or a farmer, an unemployed man or one who is employed. President Nixon's proposal would provide funds to all those whose income falls below certain levels. This is certainly a major advance.

However, the level of incomes proposed are so low

that the plan will not really begin to permit the abolition of the many other types of welfare programs now operating. It will be difficult to make real progress in abandoning the present overlapping schemes until the basic guaranteed income reaches a more adequate level. On the other hand, realistic political analysis suggests that the President may have difficulty in achieving even the proposed levels.

The most significant danger in the proposal results from the fact that all those receiving income who do not hold jobs are expected to register so that they can find jobs or receive training. This decision alone would vitiate any advantages in the program, for all the reasons I discussed above under the disadvantages of a "guaranteed employment" approach to our poverty problem. In terms of that discussion, the chief weakness of the President's proposal is precisely its guaranteed employment direction. As I argued, we must *choose between* a guaranteed employment approach and a guaranteed income approach, whereas the President attempts to *combine* these diametrically opposed alternatives.

This chapter was adapted from a speech originally given to faculty and students at the University of Kentucky, March 3, 1969.

Communication to Build the Future Environment

Our future will not be like our past. But what alterations are inevitable and which should be avoided, what routes can we use to create a more human future and which are blocked? These questions are still profoundly controversial and there are no accepted answers. We do know that man is achieving the power to alter fundamentally the physical environment in which he lives. It is also clear that he does not yet know how to control this power nor how to calculate the consequences of the actions he decides to take.

"whatever direction progress takes . . . will be a dramatic one"

In the past, man has concentrated on gaining the power to do what he wished; now he must decide what he wishes to do out of the enormous range of options open to him. That is, today's institutional structures were not designed for facilitating choice; rather, they were designed to increase man's domination over the physical environment. Therefore, if man is to survive we must work together to create new methods and institutions to decide on our goals. This statement is one step toward understanding the substance of the problem and the approaches that can and cannot be used to build the future and to create the new institutions we require. The new technologies we have created do not, of course, promise utopia; rather, by making it possible for us to provide for man's material needs, they force us to consider not only how our new potentials can be realized but also man's inherent possibilities and limitations.

PRODUCTION SOCIETY/INFORMATION SOCIETY

Western societies have moved in recent centuries toward an "objective" view of life. As we move toward a society based on communication this viewpoint is increasingly challenged. "Objectivity" is not possible; each person sees the world differently. We are discovering that there are many modes of communication beside the mind; the value and worth of many of them are still controversial both in terms of their desirability and their potential. We, therefore, are understanding that conventional, objective teaching methods and their recent developments into programmed learning are only appropriate in certain circumstances; on other occasions it is desirable to use dialogue.[1]

Dialogue methods assume that one way people learn is in informal and open situations by grafting new knowledge relevant to them onto facts, theories, ideas and ideals already known; people engage in interchange and comparison with others they see as equals. Conventional teaching — and its extension, programmed learning — operates on the assumption that objective information can be transferred relatively intact from the programmed teaching machine, whether human or mechanical, to the human mind.

We need to discover where each of these techniques can be most effectively employed. This is extraordinarily difficult because the issues involved are not only practical but also, essentially, philosophical. The group which believes in programmed learning finds the "communication" of the other group inexcusably muddy and confused. The "dialogue" group, on the other hand, argues that the precision of the statements of those engaged in programmed learning has been achieved by excluding the most relevant issues. Thus a profound disagreement over appropriate language hinders the development of meaningful dialogue about the basic issues. Also, many of our communication problems today can be traced to a continuous confusion of levels of argument.[2] For example, we often discuss goals in terms only suitable for arguments about implementation and implementation in terms only suitable for the discussion of goals. It seems clear, however, that a synthesis must and can be achieved.

We are also confused about our aims and goals because we still do not really understand the new world into which we are moving. We do know that changing conditions have already been responsible for the collapse of the dominant liberal consensus that first began to develop in the 1930's. This consensus saw its full development in the forties and fifties; there came to be rather general agreement among intellectuals that it was necessary for the federal government to intervene in the economy and society to prevent economic recessions and to remedy social problems.

This consensus was so complete at the beginning of the sixties that it led to massive legislation. The consequent planning and policy developments have, however, proved highly unsatisfactory to many groups in the society, partly because the developments did in fact favor some groups against others and also because there was no sense of involvement by many in the process of decision-making.

TWO VIEWS

Those who have found their interests damaged by the measures adopted in the sixties are increasingly angry. If the American society is not to be split beyond repair we must develop a new basic understanding of the rights and responsibilities of human beings. We must also understand the two profound dynamics that are now emerging. These dynamics are related to, but not identical with, the conflicts which emerged in the 1968 Presidential election. There are those who feel that America will continue to develop satisfactorily if only its inherited traditions are restored; and there are those who believe that profound, rapid change is required to move us into the future. The question we must ask urgently is if it is possible to open up communications between these two groups so that the valid aspects of their arguments can be meshed and the potential for a new underlying consensus produced.

There is an urgent need for institutional structures which permit the meeting of people from all groups in the society on neutral ground. These "institutions" should be run by mature human beings who can absorb the frustrations and hatreds which will often be expressed and thus prevent them from destroying the potential of communication.

A growing number of churches, educational institutions and national organizations such as the League of Women Voters and the American Association of University Women are reaching out in an attempt to meet this challenge. One model is the American Friends Service Committee which has had a center serving this function for members of the United Nations for several years.

Creative dialogue is possible only if there is relevance within each point of view. Each of the two attitudes summarized earlier does, in fact, have valid aspects, but these valid aspects can be seen only when viewed from the perspective of a larger whole. It is true that a complete overturn of all present structures would destroy America. It is true that the widespread ignoring of the fundamental values inherited from our past is deeply dangerous. It is true that man cannot ignore the nature of the new realities if he is to survive.

These are negative statements. What can we say about the positive aspects of these two views? The lesson of the first view is that if mankind is to survive it must be aware of its genetic and historical heritage; the future can grow only out of its past for it is the shaper of the present. The lesson of the second view is that if mankind is to survive it must invent the future through its imagination; it must develop structures, languages and symbologies suitable for our new world.

We must get beyond the view that the two dynamic approaches in the United States today are contradictory; we must, in Maslow's self-actualizing terms, synergize these apparent polarities. We must come to see them as different ways of looking at the issue, "How can mankind participate in creating the future?" In today's situation we must, in particular, examine how man can benefit from the environmental and technological change that he himself has started. We must, therefore, find ways to enable communication among all active groups to ensure that the insights of each group are widely understood and the inadequacies of each stance challenged.

There has been, and indeed still is, a rather general belief that all those in the "disinherited" groups — minorities, women, the poor, the young — see the need for fundamental change and that those presently in "power structures" all want to retain the present. Those who believe in the potential of communications usually argue that there are change-agents in all classes and areas of society who can be brought to recognize each other through open dialogue and then be able to act more effectively together.

During most periods of history, the two drives — toward the past and the future — act upon a relatively "immovable" center viewpoint which is not able to be widely or rapidly changed. At the present time, however, there is a growing feeling among a very substantial part of the population that something is seriously wrong in the United States.

This is leading to polarization between the two views. Unfortunately, both the forward-looking and backward-looking stands become dangerous when isolated and placed in direct conflict with each other. We know that when any group with a particular set of values is cut off from communication with others, or cuts itself off, it tends to become more dogmatic, sterile and unproductive in its thinking. Common mechanisms cause this result: people filter out ideas which conflict with their own established beliefs; also, group solidarity becomes more and more intense and insures increasingly strong disapproval of any ideas which are not shared by the group. The individual who does not fit the thinking of the group conforms, cops out or is expelled.

There should be no need to detail the consequences if the present trend toward fragmentation should develop as far as is clearly possible. High levels of tension and violence always result when groups are so convinced of the rightness of their views that they are totally intolerant of the ideas of others. This can lead, in turn, to a growing acceptance of coercive authority even if it means the suppression of ideas needed to create the future.

BASIS AND MEANS FOR COMMUNICATION

Effective communication is required if we are to reverse the present drift toward polarization. We need to recognize, however, that getting people together to talk about issues will not necessarily lead to new understandings. Homogeneous groups normally reinforce, rather than alter, the prejudices of members. Input of new ideas is usually barred and if admitted is usually translated into something familiar and comfortable. What about heterogeneous groups, then? Leaving aside the difficulties of creating such groups, we must remember that a person hears information in terms of his own framework; therefore, remarks intended in one sense by a participant are often perceived very differently by another participant. In other words, new information alone will not necessarily bring about attitude change. "Facts" can be understood from many viewpoints. For example, the reality of poverty in the midst of abundance can be seen as a failure of the social system to provide the individual with an opportunity to develop a capacity to participate in the society. Or it can be perceived as the result of the laziness and irresponsibility of certain individuals or groups of people.

Changes in attitude and action patterns require an openness of the individual to the idea of a changing future, a willingness to learn and an acceptance of the possibility that he may be wrong and that others may be right. We must recognize, however, that this stance can be reached in two ways. Those who live in terms of a moral commitment may reach such a position in terms of the action they believe they should take; practical individuals may develop the same stance by intellectually recognizing the need to prevent deterioration which will ultimately be catastrophic.

PERCEPTION IS SUBJECTIVE

There are undoubtedly many people who want to listen and to learn but who have not been provided with the tools necessary for the task. Across the United States a wide range of techniques have been developed to help the individual find himself and develop sufficient confidence in his own capabilities to be able to confront the reality of other people's views and to work effectively within a group to achieve goals discovered through dialogue. Esalen-type groups represent one kind of approach. Also, Human Potential Seminars have made significant contributions.[3]

Information will be used only if it appears *credible* and *relevant.* The combination of these two requirements poses extreme problems in today's polarized climate where many relevant facts are simply unacceptable and therefore "in-credible" to many groups. A simple example of this problem is the range of "facts" presented in the debate over population control.

There are several methods of presenting ideas which can be effective. First, those concerned can work with an individual who is seen as relevant by a particular group, assuming that he is willing to challenge the myths on which the group presently relies. Second, people can talk about the future in such a way that the individual may be led to challenge for himself the present beliefs by which he lives. Thus projections of medical technology and consequent birth and death rates may lead to reconsideration of appropriate birth-control policies while examination of the trends of weaponry may lead to a rethinking of the relevance of war.[4] A third method which has proved successful is to provide people with "tools" with which they can record their own impressions of their environment and their reality. The availability of tape recorders to aid mentally-disturbed young people has freed them from neuroses and the provision of movie cameras to people in the slums has enabled them to see their immediate realities from the outside. Indeed, the presentation of a television or filmed program describing a particular community may have a freeing effect on all those involved as they see themselves from new perspectives.

One can also develop a basic presentation — whether film, audiotape or book — in which a wide range of alternative views are sharply focused. These should cover the full spectrum of all those likely to take part in the discussion, so that each individual can be provided with material on which he can base his arguments. The many attempts to use this model up to the present time have usually been weakened by a failure to cover a sufficiently broad spectrum of opinion and by failures to follow up with adequate time, money and personnel.

Involvement in a joint action program is often the best way to bridge gaps in understanding. New insights and attitudes can become permanent when the individual is given the opportunity to confirm them in action. The acceptance of an action program permits differences to be submerged in the drive toward a common goal; after a time the differences may appear less crucial because misunderstandings are overcome as those in the group communicate with each other and as new agreements emerge. A fascinating example of this approach occurred when a group of high-level lawyers were asked to "help out" in the lower criminal courts. They were so shocked by the conditions they found there that they worked effectively across ideological boundaries to bring about changes.

There can be no doubt, however, that effective communication techniques that lead first to common understandings, then to regroupings of peoples and then to actions that provide communities with power over their lives must necessarily lead to severe clashes before new structures appropriate to our new time are established. As local communities learn what they need for their own development, they discover that they are hampered not only by existing ideological structures but also by existing institutional structures — management, labor, education, government and religion. The effective realization of cooperation within a community will often lead to conflict within the present societal structures. This conflict, however, can often help to provide the climate in which there is a willingness to create meaningful change. The clash between the educational board, the teachers union and the experimental Ocean-Hill Brownsville school district can only be understood in these terms. The desire of the experimental school district to work with teachers who were genuinely attuned to the needs of black students clashed with the established patterns of job security of the teachers union and the bureaucratic patternings within the school board.

Attempts to understand and solve the conflicts which are developing as communities demand a right to structure conditions are greatly complicated by the fact that the various parties to such disputes inevitably use different words to express the same meanings and, even more seriously, belong to several different social structures with profoundly varying aims and institutions.

In this connection, we must recognize the fundamental difference in the position of those against whom the society is discriminating and those for whom the society appears satisfactorily organized. Those who feel the need for change most — minority groups, women, the poor, the young — will usually be least patient with the process of dialogue and will be unwilling to participate unless there is clear-cut evidence of the potential for meaningful action. Those who need change least have, in the past, often called for dialogue and used it to prevent the meaningful action so urgently required. Effective dialogue between the powerless and those in power structures can be a means to prevent breakdown and violence, but only if it results in rapid and realistic change.

KNOWLEDGE AND NEWS

The mass media have largely failed to tackle the difficult problems involved in moving information about the controversial issues of the day; even their best efforts have been flawed by failure to provide opportunity for feedback. This is largely because they have perceived reality in terms of objective "facts" and "trends" and have not developed techniques to deal with subjective controversy about goals nor about the ways of creating new potentials for the future. In addition, their structure as profit-making businesses and vehicles for merchandising goods has limited their potential as change-agents.

One of the fundamental issues which must be reconsidered is the meaning of news in modern society. Essentially, news today means bad news; we are concerned with the areas of breakdown in society. We are surely in urgent need of a redefinition so that news not only includes good news as well as bad news but also encourages us to look for the causes of breakdowns in society. Any redefinition of news should not equate bad news and controversial matter. There is a need for massive movement of valid but controversial ideas; we must find ways to overcome the present extremely efficient barriers.

One key issue here is the role of the government in the movement of information. We recognize that perception is always subjective. We must ask to what degree governments can move information without distorting it for their own ends. Should governments see the provision of means for information movement as a free service? If there is to be more massive involvement of the government, how should competition between free, public information and purchasable, private information be arranged? And how should any division of responsibility be made effective?

A second key issue is the need to reconsider the present structuring of social science knowledge. We have assumed up to the present time that reality can best be understood when divided among disciplines: economics, sociology, political science, etc. Real problems, however, can be solved only by using knowledge from all the disciplines.

It is often argued that we should re-structure knowledge around problem areas. If this is to be possible, we must develop new frameworks of analysis. One of the most promising which now exists is called the dialogue focuser. In it the areas of agreement are first established, then the areas of disagreement as well as the reasons for the disagreement. Disagreement usually depend on different views about facts, trends, the nature of man, the nature of the environment and the goals and aims of the good society.

Dialogue focusers provide the individual with enough information to permit him to enter the debate at the point of real present concern rather than concentrating on issues which have already been decided. The format could be computerized as our skills develop further and it would then be possible to keep the statement permanently up to date. As disagreements were resolved and new problems discovered, the statements could be rapidly changed. In addition, statements could be prepared at various levels of difficulty and complexity; some people need all the available detail and others only the general outline of a topic.

The preparation of such statements will often require the creation of special centers devoted to specific topics. Some centers of this type are already developing; the creation of others should be encouraged. It is essential that we learn to find new ways to "institutionalize intelligence," to insure that those who understand the potentials of the future can be effective. Several centers which fall roughly within this category can be cited: the Center for the Study of Democratic Institutions at Santa Barbara, the Center for Social Pathology at Iowa Wesleyan and the Center for Urban Care at Augsburg College.[5]

NEW PATTERNS

We must consider what number of people can communicate effectively to create the agreement required for human living and what types of decision should be handled on what levels. Profound changes in patterns of local, regional and international communication will be required.

For example, we need to re-examine the belief that the large city — or the megalopolis — represents the predominant development of the future and that the depopulation of rural areas will necessarily continue. The requirements for effective communication suggest that we must encourage the development of local communities. While decisions about the overall direction of the area and region can and must be effectively reached, there is also a need for each small community in the city and each town and village in rural areas to have a possibility of local goal setting. The drive toward decentralization which is occurring in the big cities is based on a sense of this necessity.

The growing drive toward decentralization is itself responsible for the breakdown of many existing communication channels and makes more urgent the intelligent use of our new communications possibilities. If man is to take advantage of the technologies he has created, he will have to learn to communicate across massive cultural barriers in spite of the growing distrust throughout the country and the world.

Lying behind all the issues so far discussed is a more

fundamental question. Is "communication" simply a novel catchword or does it represent a new understanding of the nature of the world in which we are going to live? The industrial age was based on a fragmentation of society into competing individuals and groups. It was assumed that this process would encourage, and force, the intelligent, dynamic action required for human development. The underlying theory behind the communication model suggests that we now need to develop a new social order based on process and cooperation rather than on force and competition.

---

the possible is irrelevant
so it is only worth trying
for the impossible

This conclusion derives from the views of leading thinkers in various fields in the social sciences who argue that man must achieve far higher standards of behavior. In effect, the new social science knowledge validates the insights of the religions for it shows that honesty, responsibility, love and humility are minimal necessities for the future if the human race is to continue to develop.

Communication provides the possibility for the reflection of these values in dialogue and action. The inherent logic of the communication process will permit us to understand how we can change obsolescent institutional structures without destroying the necessary cohesion in the community. Most of the knowledge we need is now available but we still lack the desire to learn how to communicate effectively. There is an urgent need for the creation of a coalition designed to discover the potentials of the new era we are entering and their translation into reality through effective action programs.

PROPOSALS

In conclusion, let us note some proposals which point toward implementation of the ideas put forth above, understanding of course that they are complementary to the rest of this chapter and the rest of this book.

1. The critical but long-range project is the linking up of the mass media's power to move information on a national scale with the potential of churches, voluntary agencies and other agencies to create small groups to discuss this information. Activity on a national scale is essential if there is to be real success in altering present attitudes. The Urban Coalition, leaders of business and labor, voluntary agency heads and those in the mass media need to work closely together if this task is to be achieved. It is hardly necessary to state that such collaboration will require major developments in the attitudes of all groups.

2. City, area-wide and regional projects should be developed to provide experience which can feed into and reinforce the eventual national program. Suf-

ficient work has now been done to insure that small towns as well as cities can develop meaningful communication programs. In addition, conferences on the theme of communication might be held on a smaller scale in different parts of the country to spread the knowledge already available. The proposals by the Kerner Commission for Urban Communication Institutes and the support by President Nixon for a nationwide series of Town Hall Conferences demonstrate the growing recognition of need for new institutions designed to support research, to encourage participation and to facilitate communication.

3. There should be far closer collaboration between the commercial and educational networks and their affiliates in relating national issues to local situations. For example, after the presentation of a national problem/possibility issue, stations could take time to set the issues in their own local setting. Thus a national introduction to the issue of the aging could be followed by a program on the problems and opportunities of life for the old in the local area. This might be done even within the typical half-hour framework; the national introduction might last only five minutes. Some of the most exciting work in this field should be accomplished through local public television stations either producing their own programs or working in collaboration with the Public Broadcast Laboratories and National Educational Television. The response to these local shows could provide critically useful feedback for further national efforts.

4. Imaginative sound and visual presentations of ideas on a wide range of subjects which would interest the citizen should be developed. In many cases, the argument can be most effectively carried by juxtaposition of images, sounds and ideas rather than by closely reasoned arguments. Films and tapes of this type should be commercially profitable; all that is needed is a wider understanding of the potential in this area.

5. Catalogs of audio-visual and written materials about specific subjects such as poverty, health, etc., should be prepared. Listings should cover material from all media, should be classified as to difficulty and should avoid the academic syndrome of listing more material than can possibly be used effectively. While it is true that there is profound resistance to use of canned material by many teachers who fear being replaced, it is also true that many teachers would use far more audio-visual aids if they were easily available. The American Library Association might appropriately take on this continuing task.

6. Packets of materials at various levels of difficulty on particular topics should be compiled. Such packets should have built into them the experience we have gained in developing leadership and improving human relationships so that the material can be used even in the absence of experienced group leaders. The packets should be designed so that they challenge people to act.[6]

7. The accepted scope of the public library should be dramatically widened. The citizen must be provided with adequate information not only through books and records but also through tapes and films. Public libraries should be linked to regional centers which would make available not only tapes and films but also the equipment on which they can be played. This is particularly critical for more isolated areas. For example, the Department of Radio-TV of the Nebraska Council of Churches is proposing the creation of approximately thirty media centers located in those Nebraska communities with a broadcast station. Each center would have a viewing room and video-tape library and be equipped with two video-tape recorders, cameras and monitors, film, slide and overhead projectors, cassette recorders, etc.

The centers would ideally be located in the public library: libraries have staff personnel for day, night and weekend access, libraries are equipped for checking out materials and civic groups are more likely to support a center when located in library vs. church or school. Schools could use equipment and facilities during the day and churches nights and weekends; church/school cooperation in a media center might help break down school/community barriers.

It is clear that these facilities will only be effectively employed if people are provided with knowledge about the potentials and limitations of the various methods: 16 mm., 8 mm., slides, tapes, stills, etc.

In towns where cable TV is available or there are other unused communication channels, the public library and other agencies can develop and schedule programming on subjects of interest. It is not essential that such programs be slickly produced if the content has integrity and is of interest to the audience which is attracted. Cable TV is clearly one of the major instruments which will revolutionize communication potentials through its extraordinary capacity to link citizen to citizen and citizen to information. We are in urgent need of intelligent policy development in this area.

[1] For a further analysis of these points see *Dialogue on Technology* and *Dialogue on Education*, Bobbs-Merrill, 1967.

[2] For a further discussion of levels of debate see Robert Theobald, "Policy Formation for New Goals," in *Social Policies for America in the Seventies*, Doubleday, 1968.

[3] See Working Appendix on Human Potential Seminars.

[4] See Working Appendix on Audio-Visual Materials.

[5] See also Working Appendix for various centers.

[6] A packet of material on the subject of Human Rights, for example, is presently being developed through funding provided by The American Lutheran Church. For information write: Loren Halvorson, Board of College Education, American Lutheran Church, 422 South Fifth Street, Minneapolis, Minnesota 55415. Work is also being carried forward by the

150

Division of Education for Mission, National Council of Churches, 475 Riverside Drive, New York, N.Y. 10025.

This chapter was adapted from a statement, written principally by Robert Theobald, which developed out of the Communication to Build the Future Environment Conference, sponsored jointly by Town Meeting, Inc. and the American Institute of Planners, held in Minneapolis, November 20-22, 1968.

Man's power has become so great that he must make intelligent choices about what he wants to do.

The growing howl about pollution, the environment and ecology threatens to lessen, rather than increase, the prospect of mankind's survival. If this chorus of concern is to result in intelligent choices then its directions must be fundamentally changed. I am in no way denying the critical nature of the ecological crisis. I am arguing that the increasing hysteria threatens to damage our chances of dealing with its realities.

Until late in 1969, concerns about pollution and the environment were confined to a small, intense group. Now this issue is the prime concern of many Americans. Vociferous arguments for prevention of pollution and preservation of the environment are becoming essentials for any aspiring politician or intellectual in good standing.

It is obviously felt that there is everything to gain and nothing to lose by stands on these issues. Republicans and Democrats are vying for the right to claim ownership of them as election issues.

There is increasing evidence that attention on college campuses is moving away from the Vietnam war to concern about pollution. A series of teach-ins, focused in the spring of 1970, evoke passions similar to earlier war teach-ins.

Newspapers across the country have entered the anti-
-pollution battle. Readers are invited to cooperate in
reporting and in eliminating sources of smoke and
solid particles.

At first sight, such developments appear completely
valuable. Man's health, man's production and his very
survival depend upon the retention of pure air to
breathe and pure water to drink. Both of these are
threatened today. Indeed, the anti-pollution-pro-
environment issue has the potential to unite the
people of the United States — and indeed the world
— if developed intelligently. Unfortunately, given
present patterns and understandings, the movement
will rapidly become divisive.

The ecology issue
can unite — or divide — us

We are failing to recognize this reality because it is
impossible to be against a good environment any
more than it is wise to declare against God, mother or
country. However, once the rhetoric of anti-pollution
is translated into specific measures there will be profound opposition — because of the more fundamental
implications of ecological thinking of justified diver-
gencies between priorities and of the pressures of
special interest groups.

Our present position on the environment issue is similar to that at the beginning of the war on poverty: who could be *for* poverty? However, the actual measures required for its abolition proved so divisive that the war died before it had really begun. The same threat lies ahead for the environmental issue — for many of the same problems are inherent in it — unless we change direction.

Many of those who are most concerned about pollution, environment and ecological issues would agree that division on this issue is inevitable. They see the pollution problem as caused by selfish industrialists, land owners, etc. whose actions can only be controlled by an aroused public opinion.

The college teach-ins were designed to create the sort of pressure which firms, cities and states cannot ignore; to force changes in priorities and spending in order to reduce water, air, land and noise pollution. Those who are most honest admit that the direction of such pressures is often ill-advised. The actors have insufficient understanding of the real problem/ possibilities of our time. However, most of those promoting the teach-ins see the crisis as so threatening and imminent that they are prepared to risk mistakes.

The analogy is made with Vietnam. It is argued that if pressures from college campuses and other aroused people could cause moral outrage and thus reverse the course of a conflict in Asia, surely it can also be used to change policies at home.

Both the analysis and the analogy are wrong. It is folk mythology to believe that the course of the Vietnam war has been changed by leftist pressure which led Americans to see the war as immoral. The war itself has not become shocking to most Americans — the overall reaction to My Lai shows this. The key factor which changed minds was that the war came to be seen as unsuccessful and expensive. Americans — particularly those in the "establishment" — found that it was interfering with more immediate priorities.

The reality unperceived by those who would repeat Vietnam-style pressures is that protest against Vietnam, and the violence associated with it, has actually reduced the chance of successful social change. There is a strong reactionary movement in this country today and its influence could only be increased if ecologists and conservationists interpreted public concern as providing them with a mandate to interrupt the operation of industries and services polluting the environment.

In addition, the problem is far more complex than the present rhetoric admits. All too often pollution is simplistically associated with technology: it is assumed that the way to get rid of pollution is to get rid of technology. Inherent in much of the literature about the ecological crisis is a nostalgia for earlier times. The magazines in their attempt to summon up a vision of an unpolluted world show us young, beautiful couples with their children — and an un-touched landscape.

This is totally unrealistic: continuation of this ap-proach can all too easily create a neo-Luddite revolt. Just as Britons smashed machines in the early nine-teenth century to avoid progress, so Americans may try to turn off their technology in order to return to an earlier agricultural state. Such an attempt would certainly create confusion and hardship; it would, of course, fail eventually. Such a diversion from the real issue, however, might well rob us of our final chance to deal with the still-growing gap between the economic and technological situations of the abun-dance and scarcity regions. We have little time left if the growth of population in the scarcity areas is not to overwhelm the total resources of the world.

The ecological crisis is indeed the central concern of our time. We must learn how to feed, clothe and shelter the population of the world while preserving their dignity and without destroying the climate and resources which make life on earth possible.

We could be brought to understand this basic issue by examining the *real* implications of the discomfort and hardship being caused to Americans by air, water, land and noise pollution. The imminent danger is that our justified concerns about pollution will cause us to turn inward and forget the immediate needs of the rest of the world.

We have hardly begun to examine the implications of the ecological crisis on a realistic scale, and as the hysteria mounts it seems even less likely that we shall do so. Today we are only able to state that our present economic, social and political institutions are totally unequal to the task.

Ecologists are presently planning to use old-fashioned divisive political techniques to achieve their goals. This divisiveness will not only hold back the realization of the most urgently required reforms but will also make it impossible to teach the deeper lesson inherent in ecological thinking.

Man's survival in the future depends on his giving up the attempt to dominate nature and learning to co-operate with it. Similarly man can only survive with other men if he abandons the present stress on competition and learns to cooperate with others. Ecologists can only hope to achieve their goals in such a cooperative world. If they continue their planned programs, they will themselves by their acts block the development of precisely the cooperative world needed.

This chapter was adapted from an article which originally appeared in the Los Angeles *Times,* February 8, 1970.

In 1967, I wrote an article in which I argued that we had to discover an educational system in which the student could fully participate. I closed with a statement of urgency: "The time for change is now, because the potentials are here and the dangers are here. If individuals and groups do not move, do not use their resources, we soon may not be able to move! This society can close down, can become unchangeable, and can become — to put it bluntly — *evil*. The choice is ours."

STRUCTURAL CHANGE

Any relevant examination of the current situation must start from a clear perception of the fact that the evolution feared has become reality in large part, and that the clearly foreseeable course of events shows that things must be expected to worsen further before we can hope for improvement. One need only look at the various polls to see how public sympathy is moving away from those who perceive the necessity for massive change and toward those who wish to restore law and order based on norms which have been made irrelevant by the massive technological revolution which man has created.

What has happened? In the earlier years of this decade the issue confronting the society was generally defined in terms of discovering how it would be possible for those who were excluded from the benefits accorded to the majority of the society to participate fully. However, when we studied and acted on this issue, we discovered that it is impossible to provide full participation for all without fundamental structural change in the society. Today, therefore, we are confronted by a growing demand from the various powerless groups — racial minorities, the poor, the young, the aged and women — that society should be so reorganized that such groups not be prevented from controlling the conditions of their own lives.

This evolution of the key domestic issue is leading to a fundamental change in patterns of alliances. The "liberal" no longer perceives the justice of the demands being made. He believes that there are adequate channels of communication available in the current society and that the structure is basically sound. He is, therefore, outraged at the fact that groups have felt it increasingly necessary to move outside accepted channels to dramatize their cause. While he was prepared to accept the fact that blacks had legitimate grievances leading to volatility and anger, he finds the "up-tightness" of students to be without real basis and he applauds measures to control it. The statement made by Father Hesburgh at Notre Dame and the general reaction to it clearly dramatize this reality.

The new alliance, which is only now beginning to develop, includes all those who perceive the need for structural change — even though disagreement still exists about the nature of the structural change which is required. This alliance sees itself confronted by structures designed to prevent meaningful change in the society. It argues that this is inevitable because bureaucracies were designed to eliminate the "human element" in decision-making. People are no longer seen as the enemy; rather, this new alliance sees the problem related to the "roles" in which people are trapped. Therefore, those involved in the alliance work to free individuals to enable them to act in new ways which seem more valuable to them.

The new alliance views the present crisis as a fact of life — recognized but essentially taken for granted. Instead of trying to hold back the incoming tide of repression, like King Canute, it is determined to ensure that the new institutions it is creating are built on rock and not sand. The alliance is concerned, therefore, to create viable models of life styles for the future world in the hope that as these styles become visible they will change the tide of public opinion. Again, to use the King Canute analogy, the alliance is interested not in preventing the tide from coming in but in changing the position of the moon so that the tide of repression will recede. But in order to produce viable new models of education and in order to influence public opinion, it will be necessary to understand appropriate educational theory for a world of permanent change. We must learn how to teach people to be able to make decisions for themselves rather than making decisions on the basis of structured authority.

EDUCATION AND TRAINING

In order to clarify the issues involved, I would like to offer a definition of the meaning of education which

I find particularly helpful: Education is the process of providing each individual with the capacity to develop his potential to the full. This requires that we enlarge the individual's perceptive ability by providing a sufficiently wide range of societal environments so that the talents of all can be used.

*Education is the process
of providing each individual
with the capacity to develop
his potential to the full*

Perhaps this definition can best be enlarged upon by once again discussing the difference between education and training — a difference which has been so muddied as to have become meaningless. Education should be seen as the process of providing the individual with the skills to participate in the ongoing development of the activity in which he is concerned. In other words, he does not need to apply a rote set of rules but rather to understand the principles which are involved in his activity. Training, on the other hand, provides a set of hard and fast rules which can be applied to a given range of situations but which do not permit further development of skills. An individual who is "educated" is able to adapt to change; an individual who is trained will find his knowledge becoming obsolete as change occurs.

There is a peculiar, and far from obvious, consequence of the definition given above. That is, the individual's purpose in trying to master a particular area of knowledge determines whether he is engaged in education or training, rather than any objective set of criteria. For example, let us look at the possible relationships between foreign languages and knowledge of the automobile. An automobile engineer desires to be educated in his chosen field because his future growth depends on a sufficiently complete understanding of the automobile to be able to participate in its further development. Therefore, he will learn foreign languages as a skill to enable him to learn more about his chosen subject: the automobile. On the other hand, the student of Romance languages will wish to be *educated* in foreign languages and to be *trained* in the use of the automobile.

Refusal to accept the fact that education depends on purpose results from snobbery: a feeling that there is a hierarchy of values in activity patterns. In other words, it is based on the belief that an "academic" is definitely and *inherently* more valuable than an automobile engineer or a gardener. If we are to be able to create an educational system valid for the future, we must accept that the area seen as education *by the individual* will depend on his own purposes. This implies, in turn, that there must be many styles of educational institutes for the many educational purposes which exist now and for the even wider range which will come into existence as we encourage the diversity made possible by the new technologies.

The problem confronting us at this point, however, is the process by which education, in the definition given above, can be achieved. We are increasingly aware of the routes available for training people in skills. Programmed teaching machines — and to an even greater extent, programmed computers — will provide the best possible individualized instruction for each person. The necessary information can be so structured that each individual can proceed at his own pace and follow his own perception of his own needs. However, we know very little about the ways in which "education" in the full sense given above can become reality. The remainder of this statement will, therefore, concentrate upon the justification for fundamental changes in the educational system and some of the initial steps which could be taken to achieve movement toward a more adequate educational system.

We get an initial sense of the areas of concern by examining the feeling on campuses across the country that the main problem which exists is that students are cut off from both relevance and involvement. The meaning of these complaints becomes clear in the light of the discussion above because the student is quite simply stating that his education is not being structured around his own educational purposes, but rather around a structured curriculum which serves the needs of departments, disciplines and administrations.

This concern can be made more concrete as we examine the two basic realities of present patterns of knowledge. First, they are static and not dynamic. The disciplines in which most students work lack a sense of the continuing evolution of the issues in the theoretical and the real world. Textbooks and teachers are more concerned with teaching the present set of conclusions derived from the present set of assumptions than with providing the student a sense of the ways in which both assumptions and conclusions have changed over time, let alone with providing the student the set of tools with which he can participate in the further evolution of the subject. To put it bluntly, most teachers are insufficiently sure of their own competence to be prepared to welcome their students as joint creators of knowledge and therefore do not provide them with the tools to surpass them. The good teacher, on the other hand, knows no greater moment than the one when a former student reaches the point where he can teach the former teacher. In other words, education has not yet caught up with the fact that the educational pattern of the past, in which it was assumed that the old know and the young must learn, is no longer valid. So long as the speed of change was relatively slow, this was a perfectly valid assumption. An entire society could be structured around a prestige structure, a knowledge structure, in which the old passed on knowledge and the young simply received it. But the enormous speed of change in our time, brought on by the cybernetic revolution, necessitates a total change in this structure.

Second, the styles of academic learning and teaching are so structured that they exclude the relevance of emotion. It is assumed that the introduction of emotion will inevitably destroy the validity of the work. It is not yet realized that there is a critical and rather simple distinction which can and must be drawn. Goals and purposes are not objective — they depend upon subjective reasoning about what is important to the individual and the group. Once goals have been set, then it is possible to analyze objectively what should be done to reach these goals. The decision to preserve the objective, analytical style of the university, therefore, means that the individual can be involved only in the "how" and not in the "why." There are many who would argue that the university should be concerned only with "how" — that it is not a place for the discovery of partisan views but for the analysis of alternative possibilities. There are two problems with such an approach. The first and most obvious is that there will always be an overwhelming tendency to analyze how to achieve the goals which already exist. The analysis of the route to these goals will then bring about a likelihood that the analyzed steps will take place and therefore bring about the goals which are presently accepted, whether they are valid or not. It is insufficiently recognized that "self-fulfilling prophecy" is one of the most fundamental of all realities: one achieves what one desires. Thus, analyses of what "might be" tend to create the possibilities which are discussed. It should be obvious that if the society has no opposing goals except those currently accepted, it becomes impossible to expect any change in the society. Thus, the decision of the university to cut itself off from subjective analysis deprives the society of one of the possible areas in which new goal creation can occur.

In addition, and even more critically, it is now clear that the brain is organized along subjective rather than objective lines. One's thought patterns are created in terms of satisfying one's own needs, and conditioned responses are created as the result of past experiences which satisfied one's personal needs. Changes in such thought patterns will occur only if the individual is brought to perceive — subjectively — that his present thought patterns do not maximize his satisfaction. In other words, it is a tautology that "each individual will always act in such a way as to maximize his satisfaction at the moment he makes a decision, given all the circumstances of which he is aware." This statement, has, of course, no content, for it applies to the individual who knocks a woman down to steal her purse as well as to the person who risks his life to capture the purse thief. Change occurs when people alter their views about which actions seem to them to "maximize their satisfaction," and this is only possible — definitionally — when their subjective views are changed.

LEVELS OF LEARNING

These points can be made clearer by an examination of theories which have been developed by Gregory Bateson, a psychologist and anthropologist now working in Hawaii. The description given below has been heavily adapted from his original work, but remains true, I believe, to his purposes. He has shown that there are various levels of learning and that each level of learning has certain structural requirements with it. The first level of learning is the simple perception of a fact. For example, an individual enters a room, and is conscious of it. The second level of learning occurs when two facts are interrelated: "When the bell rings, I go to lunch." The third level of learning occurs when an individual improves his performance within an existing system of understanding: "If I go to lunch half an hour before the bell rings, I have to stand in line but I will get good food. If I go to lunch half an hour after the bell rings, I will get my food immediately but it will be the leftovers." The fourth level of learning occurs when one is able to perceive the nature of the present systems and to reexamine them with a view to discovering how the total system can be changed. If we stay in the area of food, for example, we might wish to reexamine the nature of the human body to discover what real options there are to present, inherited patterns of eating habits, given the fact that we now need far less calories both because we are kept artificially warm and because we need to exert far less physical effort.

To what do these levels of learning correspond in real life? The first level occurs as the child reaches the stage when he can distinguish between stimuli, rather than all life being a total gestalt with no perception of differences. The second stage occurs when two realities are interconnected for the first time. For example, the young duckling discovers his mother and is then programmed by instinct to follow her. It has been shown that the "mother" can be a wide range of objects rather than the actual mother. (In this connection, it is clear that the Pavlovian experiments are simply a special case of level-two learning — that it is possible to relate any two experiences together if they are reinforced a sufficient number of times.)

The third level of learning is the one which our present systems of "education" are geared to achieve; that is, they are designed to make it possible to improve our level of performance within our present perceptions of the state of the universe. In the terminology used above, the present "educational" system is concerned with training and not education. The effect of this pattern is that people are taught about realities as they are presently perceived, and they are later placed in roles where they have no choice but to act within the current realities. The revolt against the school and university system results from the fact that there is increasingly general realization that the present understanding about the state of the social system is not valid. Though this is particularly obvious for the ghetto school where the real world is the teacher rather than those human beings playing the role of teacher, we are rapidly coming to realize that the problem is by no means confined to the ghetto.

168

FOURTH-LEVEL LEARNING

Therefore, we are beginning to perceive the need for fourth-level learning — learning which permits us to change our perceptions about the nature of the world in which we live. But while we have begun to perceive the necessity for this, we have not yet realized that the styles which make possible fourth-level learning are profoundly contradictory to those needed in third-level situations. That is, the methods which are used for training are profoundly unsuitable for real education. Given this reality, we must take seriously the particularly permanent character of our thinking because of the very nature of brain structuring and also the fact that all societies are so structured that they act to prevent fourth-level learning. This is the meaning of Arnold Toynbee's statement that cultures have not, in the past, adapted to fundamental changes in their environment. In effect, he is arguing that these cultures have never been able to achieve the fourth-level thinking which would have been necessary to enable them to change their basic understandings of the nature of the world, and to develop new patterns of structures and institutions appropriate to the new world which the society had entered. We are now going through our own "Toynbee crisis," and the decisive factor as to whether or not we can deal with it will be our ability to create the conditions for fourth-level learning.

Fourth-level learning requires that people be enabled to move outside their present perceptions of reality and to see new ones which will then enable them to discover and accept new patterns of action and behavior. Three overall routes to fourth-level learning appear to be emerging.

First, there is the wide range of processes which are being developed to help individuals, either singly or in small groups, break out of their current Skinner-boxes. The aim is to develop new patterns of goals which would enable people to begin the process of overcoming their weaknesses and thus develop their own human potential. The theory behind this approach is that it is more valuable to develop one's potential strengths than to concentrate on eliminating one's weaknesses. The Human Potential Seminar is one of the best known of these techniques.[1] It operates by freeing people to set immediately achievable personal goals and by developing the scope of these goals over the period of the seminar.

The second route is to develop a social situation in which people can join together around a common goal which is more important to those involved than the ideologies by which they presently live. It has been proved on innumerable occasions that the search for an effective strategy will cause people to develop and accept new models which will challenge their existing conditioned responses. However, it is also increasingly clear that involvement in an experience of the first type listed above may be necessary before many human beings are ready for involvement in the development of a common social purpose.

The third route is to introduce a wide range of new ideas which effectively challenge all existing idea patterns. This can be done, for example, by an imaginative speaker who attacks the "sacred cows" of all ideologies rather than a single one; and, in so doing, provides new sets of ideas to various people in the audience. It can also be done by way of the modern media — radio, film, TV — in which the content of the media production creates a new gestalt which encourages change in personal thinking. It can also be done by several people of differing views engaged in dialogue rather than sterile debate on where their views differ. In all these cases, however, it appears essential that those individuals who hear or see these presentations have an opportunity to be involved in their discussion in a significant way. Otherwise, the new input will not "stick."

It should be obvious that there is one profound similarity between the requirements for third- and fourth-level learning and two equally profound differences. The profound similarity is that every individual needs reinforcement. Each of us needs to perceive success in the terms that are important to him. The first profound difference is that the methods of measuring success change as we alter levels: success in third-level learning is measured by objective tests such as grades; fourth-level learning can be measured only by subjective measurements. The second profound difference is in terms of one's attitude toward those who are unlike oneself and do not share one's knowledge and beliefs. In objective learning it is rather

generally felt that there are certain things that everyone should know, and that it is therefore justified to
force people to learn certain things — thus the requirements for certain core curricula, etc. In fourth-
level learning, on the other hand, one realizes that
each person has a different set of areas in which he
wishes to be educated, and that it is both irrelevant
and immoral to force the individual to be involved in
courses which do not interest him. This is a recognition that one can affect only individuals who share
real interests. Therefore, rather than trying to involve
everybody with one's concerns, one should be content to work with core groups who already perceive
that they share common concerns. If the concerns are
real and important, their development over time by
the core group will lead others to become interested.
In particular, we must understand that we cannot
change a person's idea by attacking his presently held
beliefs, but we can be effective if we add new conditioned responses to those he already holds. This
means that one must involve any individual from the
point at which he now is, rather than forcing him to
share one's own set of concerns. But in order to do
this, one must be prepared to be wrong, and to accept
that the other person may be right. One must be
prepared to work within the other person's reality if
one is to have any hope of changing him.

It is for this reason that attempts at personal contact
between people who are intensely antagonistic have
no chance of success. A black separatist and a white
racist — to use two common labels — will fear enter-

ing each other's reality and each will therefore simply attack the surface symbols of the other. The necessary attempt to discover new realities so that one may engage in fourth-level learning can start only by talking to people whose ideas are sufficiently similar to one's own so that they are not too threatening. In this way, one is not afraid to try to understand fully the reality from which the other individual operates.

It is at this point that the profound clash between existing third-level (training) institutions and future fourth-level (educational) institutions becomes most acute. The process of sharing ideas cannot be limited by structural authority — authority derived from one's position. If fourth-level education is to occur, one must accept only sapiential authority — authority resulting from the individual's knowledge of the particular field under discussion and acceptance by the others involved of this authority.

It is still insufficiently understood that the tension of today does not derive from the fact of differential sapiential authority but rather from the fact that too many of those with structural authority do not possess the sapiential authority to make their decisions intelligent. Students have been — and still are — asking faculty and administration to join with them in creating new structures in which sapiential authority is the source of the necessary decision-making. I am not implying — nor, I believe, are the vast majority of students — that students hold all the sapiential authority, or indeed most of it. They are asking only for a recognition of the fact that in today's world, in which many of the young have sapiential authority simply by being nearer to the new conditions than we are, they should be allowed to participate fully insofar as they are competent. We should take seriously the statement by Margaret Mead that in today's world all those who are over thirty are pilgrims in a strange land.

The new world will not be our world
It will be created by young people
who know how to live in a new environment

In addition, I am not suggesting that we should fall into the trap of assuming that all we have to do is to inform students that we recognize that they have sapiential authority and that they should go ahead and exercise it. This statement, used by many experimental colleges, effectively guts the student, for it provides him with far more freedom than he can handle effectively. Our responsibility, instead, is to provide conditions in which the individual can come to perceive his own sapiential authority and to learn to contribute where it is most relevant. I am convinced that it is equally immoral to assume the sapiential authority before it really exists, as this is to deny the possibility of its creation.

In all our relationships with human beings we have

174

the responsibility to help them structure for themselves situations within which they grow. A useful
rule of thumb might well be "what one already
handles plus ten percent for risk." It seems to me that
this rule is as relevant for the very young child as for
the full-grown adult; the recognition of the potential
of failure if one oversteps one's capacities is as critical
for a healthy human being as the recognition of one's
enormous potential power to do what one desires.

PATTERNS TOWARD CHANGE

The creation of the possibility for fourth-level learning on the campuses across the country requires as
many different techniques as there are campuses.
Change in specific situations depends upon the
"political" realities of each campus. There are, however, some patterns which may have some general
validity and they are listed below. It is critical, however, that there should be an understanding that these
ideas can be valuable only if they are completely
subordinated to a full understanding of the nature of
the campus under consideration. There are no "cook-
book" recipes for campus change.

Problem-centered courses should be created which
combine the study of the problem with action to deal
with it. Care should be taken to study problems
which are within the competence of the student.
Otherwise, one may be destructive of the student and
worsen the problem under consideration. Few materials have been produced to support such problem-
centered courses; one initiative is the *Dialogue* Series

of books.[2]

The grading system should be eliminated over time. There are many ways of chipping away at the system: pass-fail, pass-no fail, subjective grading, class grading. It is probably relatively unimportant which route one uses so long as it is realized that the ultimate objective is to get to the point where the critical indicator is the individual's subjective view about the value of the course he took.

We should move toward courses which do not last a full semester. One might design courses which spill over into a new semester, end when the instructor determines that all possible learning has taken place, etc. In other words, work toward a set of techniques which can begin to eliminate the assumption that knowledge is necessarily fashioned in four-month chunks.

We should create a "neutral point" in which all those concerned with the future of the campus can meet together on an extended basis to discover what should be done in a setting which bars challenge to motivation and assumes commitment to change.

The nature of the student body should be changed so that the divisions between faculty and students become less obvious. This might be done by bringing in middle-aged and experienced individuals who have different visions of the society.

The university should be involved in the community so that it becomes possible to eliminate the concept that one is either being educated or one is living. It seems clear that one of the necessary changes for the next generation is that we cease to see life as being for earning and begin to see life as being for learning.

On a far more general level, I would argue that the necessary base for most of these changes is the creation of an information system which will inevitably require computers by which the student can gain information about what he needs to know immediately. As I see it, he should be able to find out about the present state of knowledge in each problem/possibility area, the range of activities now occurring on campus and the interests of others on the campus so that he can find the like-minded people with whom he could work successfully. The threat of "big brother" would be avoided if each person had the right to determine what he wanted to have put on the computer.

CHANGE THE FRESHMAN CLASS

Any or all of these steps may be relevant on a particular campus, but I still remain convinced that the most appropriate first step on many campuses is to change the nature of the incoming class. There are two important reasons for this approach. First, there is no doubt that each incoming freshman class is better informed and more "turned-on" than the one which preceded it. Second, freshmen arrive believing the campus is as the catalog says it is. If they are reinforced in this belief, their actions may succeed in creating the type of campus which is required and already described in the catalog! In addition, we should always remember that freshmen have four years to affect the campus.

There are two significant, possible patterns of action. First, one might create a new style of freshman orientation designed to discover which of the incoming students are already excited and to place them in touch with faculty who have the skills to help them develop. The process might start with the mailing of a book to all incoming students. Possible choices could include *How Children Learn* by John Holt or *Compulsory Miseducation* by Paul Goodman. Many other books would be suitable — the only requirement being that they invite thought rather than putting across completed concepts.

When the freshmen arrive on campus, one of the parts of freshman orientation could be a continuous film show designed to "blow their minds" or, more technically, randomize their synapses. The exit from the cinema would be through a room where there would be a continuous bull session so that those who wanted to talk would have an opportunity to do so.

Those who were really interested would then be offered two opportunities. First, they would be asked what they would like to learn which might not be possible within the current university setup. Courses would then be created grouping those with similar interest. We now have sufficient experience with creating free universities so that the mechanics of this process should not be difficult.

Second, there would be tables in an adjoining room where those who needed advice on which major they should take, or which courses they should take within their major, would be able to seek assistance from students and faculty members from each major field. The object would be to help students find those courses and those professors who would be most likely to provide them with the sort of education which would be relevant to them.

The basic requirement for such a freshman orientation program is that a significant number of those in senior classes be prepared to stop taking their frustrations out on the incoming students and, instead, to work honestly with them. There is also a need for a significant number of faculty to be involved if the turned-on student is not to find himself in a turned-off class.

Innovations of this type in freshman orientation have already occurred across the country, and there has usually been little difficulty in making these changes. Those in charge of freshman orientation have usually been interested. This does not hold true for the other step which appears essential if freshmen are to reach the point where they can participate fully in a meaningful university program. We need a freshman introductory year which will offer the skills necessary for involvement in fourth-level learning.

First, we need a crash course in social reality. This would be based on new developments in the sciences, the technology and the socioeconomy. Each third week, students would be provided with data about a possible development and then would be asked to brainstorm for three weeks about the importance of the development, the way in which it could best be introduced, the dangers it might involve, etc. It would be made perfectly clear that there were no "correct" answers.

The second course would be in how to think logically. This would involve the practice of such techniques as inductive and deductive logic, etc. Great care, however, would be taken to ensure that the student was not paralyzed by words. Rather, the individual would be placed in a situation where he would learn the techniques and only later discover that he had been engaged in "difficult" tasks.

The third course would teach the methods which can be used to create new ideas. One popular word for this is "grooving" — the process by which the knowledge possessed by the group at the end of a session is greater than that which was available to any single member of the group at the beginning. The technical term for this is synergy — a descriptive word for the processes which occur in nature and elsewhere which lead 1 + 1 to equal three plus.

The final course would be in perception. The freshman student would learn skills enabling him to perceive a wider range of the phenomena by which he is surrounded. At one level this is an art course. The object, however, is not to help the student appreciate existing art works, not even to help him to create art for himself — although this might be a desirable by-product — but only to learn to use his senses to widen his own perception.

We are now at the point where we will either succeed in creating and communicating new educational models or we can expect public pressure to become so great that "education" will become impossible. The educational approach which I have suggested here is not designed to force change on anyone. Rather, it believes that our only hope is to develop ideas which are inherently so powerful that they make their own way in the world. John Maynard Keynes, the great British economist, stated that sooner or later it is ideas and not men which rule the world. Our goal today must be to reduce the amount of time between the creation of an idea and its evaluation and subsequent introduction if it is proved to be valid.

[1] See Working Appendix on Human Potential Seminars.

[2] See Working Appendix on *Dialogue* Series.

This chapter originally appeared as an article in *Journal* (United Church of Christ, Council for Higher Education), April, 1969.

13 A Plea for Damaged Children

The editors of the first edition chose to include an essay of my own entitled "A Plea for Damaged Children." The essay was a rather timely one, but my time, like everyone else's, has changed. One element of that essay remains timely, however, and it is included here as a summary of the tensions between our present future and the one envisioned by Robert Theobald.

These verses were inspired by several discussions with my students concerning an observation by R. Buckminster Fuller. Bucky was once asked if he was a genius, and he replied "There is no such thing as genius. Some children are less damaged than others."

The following song was formally dedicated to Bucky on the occasion of his seventy-third birthday.

Noel McInnis

Most every newborn babe in this universe is put together mighty fine.
Though one of millions conceived in nature's bountiful purse, he's the only one of his kind.
Born for perfection, given over-protection, he's boxed in body and mind.
Born to be him, he's raised to be us, and we put him in a lifetime bind.

We've gotta let grow our little children, 'cause verbs weren't meant to be nouns.
Yeah, children are a whole lot like people that way, and we've gotta stop puttin' 'em down.

A six-year-old child is brought into school, where we tell him what he doesn't know.
We tell him what we're gonna tell him, then we tell him, then we tell him that we told him so.
Born for creation, not regurgitation, he diligently wilts in his row.

Born to think his thoughts, he's stenciled with ours, and made to be someone he won't know.

We've gotta let know our growing children, 'cause verbs weren't meant to be nouns.

Yeah, students are a whole lot like people that way, and we've gotta stop puttin' 'em down.

Graduation comes, the student's on his way, he can start to be a human being.

But he'll only have a couple hours a day when he's not serving some machine.

Born for relations, it's for manipulations his life is rewarded so green.

Born to do his thing, but doing a thing's thing, he seldom gets a chance to mean.

We've gotta let go our grown-up children, 'cause verbs weren't meant to be nouns.

Yeah, people are a whole lot like children that way, and we've gotta stop puttin' 'em down.

14 Why and How to Dialogue

Man lives today caught between the possibility of a truly human future and the possibility of unlimited catastrophe. Each one of us is trying to create his own personal understanding of the freedom gained by man's development of power over his own environment. In general terms it seems that mankind is no longer caught in a system in which he is a mere cog. Today we have the ability to free ourselves to direct the future course of Spaceship Earth within the realities we have inherited as one human race from our biological past.

As we have seen, we are moving from one period of history to another. The earlier great changes — from the hunting-gathering stage to the acricultural stage and from the agricultural age to the industrial age — were slow and painful. Especially during the first transformation mankind had centuries and centuries to change from living off the free production of the land and the sea to controlling it for his own benefit. Further, his social practices, his economic thinking, and his religions evolved slowly. Today the difference in the pace of change is almost unfathomable as we move from the industrial era to the cybernetic era. What our ancient forefathers did over thousands of years we must experience in our society and our economy in *one generation,* and we must involve *all* the world in it.

WHY

In effect, we must move away from trying to increase

further our technological power to take actions. We must now learn to determine what we should do with the power we have today and will have increasingly tomorrow. That we shall increase our power is certain; a decision to cease to concentrate on technological change does not mean that our technological power will no longer grow, but rather that we can treat technological change as a given, built into our society. Nor does it mean that we shall no longer have a problem of choice; we will never be able to do *everything* we wish, but we have already reached the point where we can do what is most important to us. Do we need to go to the moon or to develop better methods of transportation on earth? Do we need new consumer gadgets or do we need to feed the hungry? Today, time and space are our scarcest products; this will force radical changes in our priorities.

Successful dialogue will help guarantee fruitful change.

Today invitations to join discussion groups are common: whites want to meet blacks, Protestants to meet Catholics, the middle class to meet the poor. To many it seems as though talk is replacing actions and that we are drowning in a sea of words. "We know the problems," many say. "All we have to do is to carry through certain programs and we can eliminate present social ills." Unfortunately, however, there are many factions — right and left, young and old, black and white among others — who are all equally convinced that their answers are correct. It is obvious that these groups usually do not agree. Dialogue is needed, then, if we are to create agreement about the steps we should be taking at the present time. If we should fail to discuss the issues in intelligent ways, the polarization which is already developing between groups must inevitably become more serious.

There are some who argue that change does not automatically follow from agreement. "The power structures," they argue, "make all the decisions about the area where we live, as well as national directions and international attitudes. They determine what needs to be done in terms of their own interests. We cannot change the power structures through discussion. Why then discuss?"

There are two reasons for challenging this view. First, recall Pogo's "We have met the enemy and they are we." Each of us has far more potential power than we exercise; we fail to exercise it because we do not know what we really desire and we do not therefore develop the energy required to create real change.

Second, while it is true that power structures follow their own interests, such a statement is not really significant, for it is also true of each one of us. Each person will always do the thing which seems best to him given all the circumstances of which he is aware at the time he acts. This statement applies to the person who saves a child from being run over in the street as well as to the individual who mugs a woman to get money for his dope habit. The relevant question is, *What* will seem *best* to *each* person?

If we really desire change, we must alter our own and other people's perception of their own self-interest. We may discover new patterns of thinking and behavior which make old ways of thinking and behavior obsolete and challenge us to alter our present action patterns. This change in patterns of action can be voluntary or it can be forced by the reactions of our neighbors and the laws of the society. Those in power structures are subject to the same pressures as each one of us: they can perceive better ways of behaving or they can be forced to change. Indeed, in many ways those in power structures are more constrained by public opinion than anyone else. Politicians must be re-elected if they are to survive; changes in public opinion therefore force them to alter their position, as the debate over the anti-ballistic missile showed. Businessmen can only sell a product which appears pleasant and safe; Ralph Nader forced a new stance on the automobile industry by making Congress take note of the lack of safety features on automobiles. The churches have altered their sense of priorities as the need for reconciliation has been brought home to them. The universities are seeking new structures to provide the student with additional potentials for learning, as logical pressure is brought to bear.

Is it possible, then, that we continue to blame the obstinacy of power structures because the alternative view is too destructive of our own self-image? Perhaps the barrier to more rapid change in many areas has not been an unwillingness to change in response to pressure, but rather the failure of those who are discontented with the present system to develop the ideas which would result in significant improvements if applied. This does not mean, of course, that those wanting to bring about change will ever be greeted with open arms; every human being — including oneself — resists alterations in his patterns of life, for change disturbs long-developed habits. But there is now sufficient recognition of the reality of the crisis we face that people in many parts of our society are looking for new ideas and concepts.

Discussion can lead to new and significant ideas which can be communicated. Will this truly cause change? The answer to this question depends on our view of human nature. In effect, an agreement to discuss involves a view that human beings are motivated to discover their changing needs. One must believe that others — and above all oneself — are open to a changed view of human needs and requirements, that the future can be better than the past. (Remember Maslow and self-actualization.) It is important that we not lose sight of this optimistic starting point as we discuss the dialogue. It is always easy to conclude that change of the necessary scope is impossible and thus ensure failure through our inaction.

HOW

What is to be done when one is convinced of the validity of the process of discussion, of the possibility of change, and of his own necessity to participate in the change — or is at least willing to suspend his disbelief? What do we know about the process by which change in people's views of their own self-interest takes place, with consequent change in the society? (It is essential to use the word self-interest here, although it can be misunderstood. We have seen that self-interest can be expressed at various levels of human growth, but it is always self-interest: each person will always do the thing which seems best to him given all the circumstances of which he is aware at the time he acts.)

The first reality we must recognize is how ill-prepared we are for the forms of discussion we need, for genuine dialogue. We have been exposed in the past to authoritarian learning situations in which it was assumed that one member of the group knew and that the others should learn. Dialogue, however, assumes that we are looking for new patterns, many of which may not be consciously known to any member of the group. We must therefore get beyond the basic learning patterns we have so far experienced in most cases, particularly in our formal education, where the teacher usually expects his students to ingurgitate knowledge and then regurgitate it without change. Rather we must look for a creative meshing of ideas between unique people who are all interested in the same topic and are willing to spend time together to develop their ideas and to create new patterns of action.

Most persons and groups do not recognize the fundamental difference between a situation in which one person can state what needs to be done and the profoundly new reality of today where we need the joint efforts of all if we are successfully to invent the future. Because we use an old-fashioned understanding of "education," we set up our groups in such a way that they cannot be truly effective; indeed many of the basic rules of thumb we apply in creating groups are actually counterproductive.

Let us, then, be specific and consider the reasons for which people can be expected to come together for dialogue, the very few rules we know which help to create — but do not guarantee — dialogue, and the criteria for evaluation of a successful dialogue group.

REASONS

It is always tempting to place absolute priorities on certain types of action or at least to suggest that certain steps must necessarily precede others. This fails to recognize that human beings have different needs at different times and that their growth does not follow neat, tidy intellectual lines. We need to provide as many alternate routes for personal growth as we can.

It seems as though people can be brought together for three types of purposes or for combinations of them: first, to perceive how they can personally act more effectively within the conditions in which they are living; second, to increase their understanding of the functioning of the world; and third, to decide what changes need to be made in the socioeconomic structures. These three starting points seem to cover all the possibilities, although the degree of specialization will be very different for groups of types two or three. It is also clear that any fully successful groups would involve the introduction of each of these elements.

The first type of group, devoted to facilitating individual growth, will be most likely to appeal to those who feel that their personal lives are presently unsuccessful. A number of techniques have now been created to help people to be more effective; one of the most developed is the Human Potential Seminar.[1] The Seminar operates on the assumption that people grow by developing their strengths rather than directly overcoming their weaknesses. The sessions start off by helping people to perceive what they have "going for them" and they try to create "success experiences" in planning one's personal life. This is group psychotherapy but with positive rather than negative assumptions about the nature of man; it challenges fundamentally the patterns of sensitivity training being developed, for example, by the National Training Laboratories.

The second type of group is likely to appeal to those who presently perceive their opportunities for self-development in terms of greater understanding of the universe in which they live and who perceive, however incompletely, that fuller understanding of the universe will inevitably increase their capacity to act on the use of dialogue techniques to discover the new truths in the new world in which we live.

The third style of group will involve those who are dissatisfied with various parts of the socioeconomic system within which they live, who want to understand it better with a view to changing it, and who feel that they have the action skills to help bring about change. Groups of this type, which take the total neighborhood or city as their concern, are of relatively late development and are only now learning how to mesh the specialized interests of various agencies: they challenge fundamentally all the fragmented organizations whether private or public.

Each of these three approaches is useful for the individual whose present felt needs accord with them; we must not try to choose between them. Each type of group and every experience of true individual learning must, however, recognize the constraints of the past, must hold a hope/belief for the future, and must act in the present, for it is only in this way that we can mesh the necessities of the past with the potential of the future. The future is not determined: it is created out of our actions and in light of our hopes and fears.

RULES

Groups are created for many purposes. One distinction is whether a group's goals are fixed and the only relevant question is how to achieve them, or whether a group is concerned with setting goals as well as finding means to achieve these goals. The rules which follow apply only to the latter: i.e., groups which must find out what they wish to do before they go about creating means to do it; *not* to groups which are given a set task.

Make sure that people get to know each other before dialogue starts.

This rule has often been reduced to: "Be sure to make introductions," but such a limitation destroys its purpose. Discussion of real issues requires a degree of trust, for otherwise there will be surface and superficial chatter rather than meaningful dialogue. One needs to know who one is talking to in order to perceive the range of skills and the range of concerns present in the room as well as the possible power relationships which may complicate or facilitate discussion. Each person present should spend at least one minute — and preferably five — in setting out the reasons why they are present, what they would like to achieve, and what they think they can contribute. Each person present should beware — both for himself and others — of self-depreciating comments such as "I'm Joe's wife" or "I'm just a housewife."

People will undoubtedly object that many discussions cannot be set up in such a way that they have time for lengthy self-introductions. The only possible response to this comment is that nothing significant will take place until people feel comfortable with each other and that this process cannot be rushed.

Real discussions require the commitment of significant amounts of time. The fact that this reality is difficult to deal with in our hectic world does not make it less real. If you want to teach others about the future — or learn from them — you must take the time to get to know them.

Limit the size of your group.

Experience has taught us that there is an optimum size for dialogue groups: normally eight the smallest size and twelve the largest. These limits result from the fact that with less than eight people there is not a sufficiently wide range of experience. With more than twelve people, the range of relevant experience is so great that it cannot be easily handled. (Experienced people can, of course, interact successfully even though the numbers are far greater.)

Even with this small a group the period you spend together can be broken up. Some people talk best in twos and threes; others like a larger group.

Don't have a discussion leader.

This is a piece of advice terribly difficult to implement, and not always relevant. But it is still the best single rule of thumb.

A self-aware group does not need a discussion leader, for the members of the group know how to lead their own discussion. If the group is not yet self-aware, the task of a discussion leader is to eliminate as rapidly as possible his own leadership role, to ensure that the group develops self-awareness; he should never substitute his own partial self-awareness for that of the total group.

There are, of course, ways that the discussion leader can "steer" the group toward more rapid self-awareness, but the more he uses his "authority," the slower the process will be. One way to put it is to say that the group should chart its own course with the leader participating as an equal.

Deal fruitfully with individual differences.

The "group" should draw out the silent person; one or more people should have become aware of the skills of the silent individual and ask him to comment when he will be relevant and when he will not feel it an imposition. The talkative individual, if he is really dominating the group and not acting as the most knowledgeable person in the group for a brief or lengthy period of time, should be informed of his behavior by another member of the group who knows him — or eventually by a collective explosion of frustration. The group itself will learn to determine what the relevant point is at a particular moment in time and will control itself for its own purposes — which will seldom coincide perfectly with the limited purposes of the discussion leader.

The group should be particularly alert to inherent assumptions about the skills of particular classes of people. There is a tendency often to assume that males between forty-five and sixty-five have most to contribute and thus to allow them to speak for as long as they wish while cutting off women and young people. The group as a whole should act to prevent this common pattern from developing.

Each group is different; each situation requires a different style. Those who have grown up with authoritatian styles will be lost if they are given too much freedom too rapidly. The practicable methods of creating group integration, as every other effort, must be based on the past and the future — in this case, the history of the individuals concerned and the hopes which are held for the future. The effort must be to find the immediate, feasible step which will move people the maximum distance from where they now are to where they want to be.

. . . plus ten percent for risk.

In every case, too little is irrelevant and too much is dangerous. One rule of thumb, which I have pointed to earlier, is to find ways to permit people to do what they already can plus ten percent for risk; such structuring is only possible if people know "where others are." This rule of thumb has relevance, for example, in determining who should meet with whom. If one presently holds a relatively narrow white "middle-class" point of view, it will probably be destructive for both sides if one tries immediately to understand the view of a black-power advocate, for the interaction will be both "irrelevant" and "dangerous."

One should dialogue with people whose world one can enter rather fully and by entering it enlarge one's own world. (Young people who act from their personal beliefs and not on the basis of an ideology can get to know each other far more rapidly.)

A group starts to function effectively when it has created its own collective experience to which it can refer. The way the group states this understanding may be serious but it is far more likely to be seen as a joke, a misunderstanding, a disaster turned into a success. This collective experience is often called a myth for it ceases to be the recitation of a set of facts and becomes a method of bringing the group together when it threatens to fall apart. (This is the only way a group can have cohesion if one excludes the possibility of an external threat, i. e., if the group does not exist to fight against another group.)

EVALUATION

How measure the success of your group? Don't be afraid of "failure." In our statistical society, we like to measure the number of groups created, the number who continued throughout the program, the actions taken. Unfortunately, these formulae do not accord with the reality of individual growth. People get involved in projects for many reasons, some positive and some negative. Up to now, because of our facination with numbers, we have tried to hold everybody in the group whether they were truly interested or not. The lack of enthusiasm of those who were not truly interested then always acted to limit and even destroy the potential development of those who wished to think, study, or work intensively.

A good analogy for a successful group is an atomic pile. Energy is produced when the pile goes "critical": that is to say when sufficient uranium rods are pulled sufficiently far out of a surrounding material which prevents their interaction. Similarly, a human group gives off energy when people are sufficiently freed from the negative forces which presently surround them.

But, one may object, if people leave our group we will have failed to provide them with the opportunity for learning. Such a statement, although it appears to be responsible, is in fact profoundly arrogant for it assumes that only one style of learning exists. Let us remember our elementary mathematics: two negative signs multiplied together are positive. People who interact badly with one person or a group may react well with another which we may help them find or which they may find for themselves. This is an enormously freeing vision if we take it seriously. The liberty it provides was expressed best by a young girl of seventeen who thought she was doing her "duty" by attending meetings of those with whom she totally disagreed. "You mean," she said, "it's all right to just go to those meetings where one can groove, where one likes the other people?"

The psychic energy needed to create change can be created by working with others with whom we agree or it can be wasted in battles which we cannot presently hope to settle but which will probably become irrelevant as the future emerges. Dialogue assumes that the future can only be invented when we join together to celebrate our human potential and when we accord to others the same right. We are all searching for a truth which will permit us to live creatively. Our different pasts ensure that we will reach it along many different routes.

[1] See Working Appendix on Human Potential Seminars.

Bibliography

SELECTED PUBLICATIONS BY ROBERT THEOBALD

The following volumes bear most directly on the subject of this book:

Challenge of Abundance. 1961 Potter.

Committed Spending: A Route to Economic Security (ed.). 1968 Doubleday; 1972 Swallow (revised edition, new title).

The Economics of Abundance. 1970 Pitman.

Free Men and Free Markets. 1963 Potter.

Futures Conditional. 1972 Bobbs-Merrill.

Guaranteed Income: Next Step in Economic Revolution (ed.). 1966 Doubleday; 1967 Anchor Doubleday.

Habit and Habitat. 1972 Prentice-Hall.

The Rich and The Poor: A Study of the Economics of Rising Expectations. 1960 Potter; 1962 Mentor/New American Library.

Social Policies for America in the Seventies: Nine Divergent Views (ed.). 1968 Doubleday; 1969 Anchor Doubleday.

Teg's 1994: An Anticipation of the Near Future (with Jean Scott). 1972 Swallow.

We list below some emerging initiatives revelant to the alternative future envisioned in this book. We also encourage readers to call to our attention persons, material or programs worthy of addition to this Appendix. Please send information to Center for Curriculum Design, 823 Foster Street, Evanston, Illinois 60204. It will be carefully considered for inclusion in future printings and editions of this book and/or in publications of the Center's Spaceship Earth Curriculum Project. (See note at end of Appendix concerning information available from the Center.)

EDUCATIONAL POLICY RESEARCH CENTER

EPRC illuminates the nature of basic issues, conceptualizes possible alternative futures and analyzes the means available for the achievement of policy goals and the consequences of alternative choices. This process entails several types of analyses, from the examination of basic assumptions regarding the nature of man to the creation of "future histories" to the exposition of benefits and costs in terms of particular interest groups. EPRC is receptive to unconventional approaches to problem-solving and to ways of acquiring new insights into educational philosophy and practices. It is neither a fact-gathering body nor a decision-making body, but a Center where vital information is collected and processed, where new fields are explored and innovations sought.

The function of the Center is to assist the educational community in analyzing policy alternatives whose long-range effects are of critical importance. The tasks of the Center are several:

To serve as a clearing house for relevant information and as an originator of policy thinking across the entire spectrum of education.

To explore the future problems of society and investigate the ways of meeting those problems.

To assemble existing information — research findings, expert opinions, results of experiments — and integrate them into alternative courses of action.

To seek to uncover crucial gaps in data and suggest ways in which the missing data can be obtained.

To serve as a communicator to the whole area of educational policy makers, from student to individual teacher to the Office of Education.

The Center has two offices: 1) Stanford Research Institute, Menlo Park, California 94025, and 2) Syracuse University Research Corporation, Syracuse, New York 13210.

S.E.A.S.

The Aspen Seminar for Environmental Arts and Sciences is an annual conference of individuals from the ecologically related sciences, from government, from industry and from general education, for the purpose of furthering participants' understanding of current environmental crises. For further information write Dr. Beatrice Willard, Thorne Ecological Foundation, 1229 University Avenue, Boulder, Colorado 80302.

HUMAN POTENTIAL SEMINARS

The Human Potential Seminars feature a number of

techniques designed to increase the participant's self-motivation, self-determination and self-esteem. The Human Potential Seminars proceed on the assumption that all the participants are mentally healthy individuals with vast amounts of personal potential that has been heretofore untapped. This is in strong contrast to traditional group therapy, which proceeds on the assumption that something is emotionally or psychically unhealthy about the participants. The Human Potential Seminars focus primarily on what the participant has going for him. They elicit individual discovery and immediate group reinforcement of the personal strengths, resources and success experiences of the seminar participant. Participants also learn to become highly conscious of their personal value systems and each individual is helped to integrate his value system with short- and long-range goals.

The Seminars have produced dramatic results in achieving the intended objectives with students, faculty and administrators at Kendall College and on other college campuses, and with teachers, counselors and students in elementary and secondary schools in the Chicago area. One Chicago high school, St. Mary Center for Learning, has devised a variation of the seminar which is offered to its entire student body (see address below). Austin College, Sherman, Texas has integrated a form of the seminar into a year-long Basic Decisions Program required of all freshmen (for information write David Reagan, Assistant to the President, Austin College, Sherman, Texas 75090).

Spartanburg (S.C.) Junior College has adapted the Seminars to its Summer Preparatory Program, which has achieved exceptional success in bringing initially unqualified students to college freshman performance levels (for information write Robert Couch, Dean of Students, Spartanburg Junior College, Spartanburg, South Carolina 29301).

Descriptive information on the Seminars is available from the Center for Curriculum Design (see address below), and from Combined Motivation Education Systems, Inc., 6300 River Road, Rosemont, Ill. 60018.

THE CENTER FOR CURRICULUM DESIGN/SPACESHIP EARTH CURRICULUM PROJECT

The Center is a non-profit educational foundation concerned with the development of educational materials and practices for thinking the world together, to complement the prevailing educational practices which fragment and compartmentalize knowledge and experience. The Center seeks, creates, and disseminates information on persons, organizations, projects, materials, strategies, and ideas for integrating knowledge, developing whole-earth perspectives and other ecological mindsets, and increasing the public's environmental awareness.

Several of the Center's current activities are integrated in a comprehensive program called The Spaceship Earth Curriculum Project. These activities include the compilation of a directory to the type of information mentioned above; the development of a study guide for environmental issues, *Can Man Care for the Earth*? (1971 Abingdon Press); and the publication of *Alternatives to Schools*, a directory of centers, networks, media, skills, and ideas relevant to alternative futures in education. Send pertinent information to The Center for Curriculum Design.

CENTER FOR EDUCATIONAL REFORM

The Center for Educational Reform was started in 1968 under the auspices of a Ford Foundation grant. The Center is in no way an attempt to institutionalize the new and growing "educational reform movement;" rather it is one attempt to measure the pulse of the movement and to explore in depth those questions central to all working for change: what does it mean to learn and how do we go about learning? Much time has been spent in examining the possible roles/modes of action such a Center can take in relation to the "educational reform movement." This movement is by necessity a decentralized network and its strength depends on the people in the field doing basic, daily, regional organizing. To aid this process, the Center is concerned with and serves three valuable functions: the gathering and distributing of relevant "social knowledge" and information and publications, the development of a growing list of consultants and organizers in the field and information on the work which they are doing, and the funding of programs which can help things happen around the country. The Center's newsletter is *EdCentric*; donation of $5.00 brings the newsletter. Center for Educational Reform, 2115 S Street, N.W., Washington, D.C. 20008.

ALTERNATIVES! FOUNDATION

An organization active in dealing with communal living groups across the U.S. and abroad, Alternatives! provides information dealing with communal living experiences and cooperative/alternative life styles. In order to make cooperative living a productive/creative venture, Alternatives! feels that self-development must receive a primary emphasis. Therefore, the foundation is engaged in the following activities:

a quarterly publication, *The Modern Utopian*, news and views about experimental communities, sexual freedom, radical social change, and the School of Living;
quarterly news of Alternatives! Foundation activities and meetings;
Directory of Social Change: communes and community organizations in the U.S., Canada and abroad;
Directory of Free Schools;
Directory of People seeking other people interested in experimental communities;
communal match-making services to help applicants find compatible people and groups;
seminars, encounter weekends, and training in freedom, communal living, and total sexuality.

Regular membership donation is $10 yearly which brings all the above publications and information about services. Alternatives!, P.O. Drawer A, Diamond Heights Station, San Francisco, California 94131.

VOCATIONS FOR SOCIAL CHANGE

Vocations for Social Change is a nation-wide clearing house for information about jobs which are specifically designed to stimulate social change. Every other month a directory is compiled of current opportunities to earn a living while working for basic institutional change. The job listings point the way to more humane social arrangements, research and study aimed at dealing with various social problems and direct action work geared toward alleviating or eliminating various forms of human exploitation. The kind of work varies from filing to fund-raising, from organizing to office work, from music to mechanics.

In addition to the listings, each issue of VSC contains essays describing how various social change efforts have been created or how new ideas could be implemented. The aim of VSC is not to be just a computer to match persons with jobs, but to be a catalyst to encourage people to create their own futures. Between issues of the newsletter, VSC sends out listings to job-hunters who have indicated interest in specific kinds of work or particular localities. VSC speakers and consultants are available to local groups.

The publication is distributed to people who are willing to share it with others by making it publicly available and to people who are willing to share their income with VSC. Although there are no set rates for any services, it is suggested that institutions who want to receive the publication for a year donate $10. Sample copies are available on request. Write Vocations for Social Change, Canyon, California 94516.

ST. MARY CENTER FOR LEARNING

St. Mary attempts a total change in educational environment, attitudinal and atmospheric, not architectural. Students (high school level) are engaged in analysis of urban environments by frequent excursions into the political, cultural and ethnic arena. Curricular changes include critical viewing of popular TV, its various genres, its effect on person and society. Personal development courses aim at effective growth — self-awareness, empathy, confrontation, support. Relationships are person-to-person rather than teacher-to-pupil. Students are engaged in the decision-making process, including full participation in school government. Students are respected as competent, maturing human beings, interacting and interfacing with senior members of the school community. For further information write: St. Mary Center for Learning, 2044 West Grenshaw, Chicago, Illinois 60612.

LIVING-LEARNING CENTER

The Living-Learning Center, at the University of Minnesota, is a mechanism for facilitation of off-campus and/or experimental-type study projects. Generally, the Living-Learning Center helps learners plan and carry out study activities which are not amenable to traditional academic philosophies and techniques. The Living-Learning Center attempts to facilitate the creation of a community of learners capable of sharing project ideas and experiences.

At present, Living-Learning Center project activities include: community live-in programs, community design study centers, "Intercultural Education Specialist" (teaching) program, Teacher Service Corps (Bachelor degree graduates with special teaching duties), special community communication programs, a Field Study Center in Honduras, credited student travel projects, along with the many more individualized kinds of activities. Write: Living-Learning Center, University College, University of Minnesota, Minneapolis, Minnesota 55455.

WORLD GAME

The World Game is an attempt to establish ways of using the world's resources to take care of everyone at an adequate standard of living, without anyone's profiting from or impeding anyone else. The Game is designed to facilitate the discovery of exponentially more efficient ways of allocating, transforming, and utilizing the world's resources so as to never decrease anyone's existing individual advantage, while at the same time making mankind 100 percent physically successful in terms of adequate living standards.

The original World Game, under the direction of R. Buckminster Fuller, has been discontinued, but world gaming experiences for college credit are being offered by another group near Detroit. They include special January and summer school courses for students who wish to transfer credit to their own colleges. Write: World Game, Duns Scotus College, 20000 West Nine Mile Road, Southfield, Michigan 28075.

CENTER FOR HUMANISTIC EDUCATION

CHE is currently completing two comprehensive directories to the human growth movement: 1) *The Eupsychian Network* will catalog all areas of what is being called "the human potential movement," in terms of places, leaders, schools, organizations, bibliography, and tapes and films available. Included will be: encounter groups, sensory awareness, T-groups, Gestalt therapy, Psychosynthesis, bio-energetic analysis, Zen, Yoga, Sufi wisdom, T'ai Chi, ESP, Transpersonal psychology, and other forms of self-actualization. 2) *Toward a Guide to Humanistic Education* will be an annotated directory to major resources in the area of humanistic and affective education: books, centers, clearinghouses, projects, consultants, curriculum materials, associations, journals and newsletters, and a media guide. Send pertinent information and inquiries to John T. Canfield, CHE, University of Massachusetts, Amherst, Massachusetts 01002.

RADICAL RESEARCH CENTER

The Radical Research Center indexes over two hundred publications that present an alternative/critical view of the institutions of American society. The *Alternative Press Index,* a guide covering publications ranging from *Dissent* to the *Leviathan* to the *Guardian* is similar in format to the *Reader's Guide to Periodical Literature* or to the *Index to Little Magazines.* A national network of indexers covers publications from their local area. The Center provides a quarterly compilation of this data by topic. The

Alternative Press Index costs $10 per year; institutional subscriptions are $30 per year. Radical Research Center, Bag Service 2500, Postal Station E, Toronto, Ontario, Canada.

THE WHOLE EARTH CATALOG

The Whole Earth Catalog, published quarterly from 1969 to 1971, and now generally available only in its final edition, The Last Whole Earth Catalog, functions as an evaluation and access device. A Sears, Roebuck type catalog, the Catalog stresses the power of the individual to conduct his own education, find his own inspiration, shape his own environment, and share his adventure with whomever is interested. Subject areas the Catalog covers include: Understanding Whole Systems, Shelter and Land Use, Industry and Craft, Communications, Community Nomadics, and Learning. The Last Whole Earth Catalog was published by The Portola Institute, 558 Santa Cruz Avenue, Menlo Park, California 94024, and distributed by Random House; it is available in bookstores at $5.

OUTSIDE THE NET

Outside the Net describes itself as a large group of friends and correspondents, and a small staff that analyzes the present educational system in hopes of facilitating its restructuring or demise. "We welcome contributions from all viewpoints and recognize that loving criticism is a necessity for growth." Subscriptions are $4 for two years. Address: Box 184, East Lansing, Michigan 48901.

DIALOGUE SERIES

To aid the transition from monologue on specialized disciplines to dialogue on meaningful issues, a series of paperback books is being issued by Bobbs-Merrill Company, Inc., 4300 West 62nd Street, Indianapolis, Indiana 46268. Presently available at $1.25 each are *Dialogue on Technology, Dialogue on Poverty, Dialogue on Youth, Dialogue on Women, Dialogue on Science, Dialogue on Violence* and *Dialogue on Education.* These books are valuable for formal and informal discussion groups of all types, as well as for high school or college classes.

AUDIO-VISUAL MATERIALS ON IMPLICATIONS OF THE NEW TECHNOLOGIES

Four films entitled "Choice," which portray the alternative futures discussed in the present volume, are available from the Broadcasting and Film Commission, National Council of Churches, 475 Riverside Drive, New York, New York 10027. The cost of rental is $10 per film or $30 for the set. Descriptive literature and study guides are available.

TEG'S 1994

This futuristic novel takes a backward look at the remainder of the century via a series of dialogues. The initiator of these dialogues is Teg, a young woman recipient of a George Orwell Fellowship which was established ten years previously in celebration of the fact that 1984 was not as bad as it might have been. The Fellowship entitles Teg to travel anywhere in the world to interview persons of her choice, the objective being to help her define her life-purpose. Her understanding of the cultural and personal fragmentation which the human world has sustained by 1994 motivates her to join with those who wish to establish the year 2000 as the beginning of mankind's period of global cooperation.

Copies of this novel by Robert Theobald and Jean Scott are available in bookstores at $6 (cloth) or $2.50 (paper), or from the publisher, Swallow Press, 1139 South Wabash Avenue, Chicago, Illinois 60605.

NEW SCHOOLS EXCHANGE

This group publishes a periodically updated directory to free schools (Summerhill type) and other experimental education endeavors, as well as a *Newsletter* which provides descriptive and analytical data on individual schools. The *Newsletter* also publishes job applications for those seeking employment in free schools. The directory and *Newsletter* are available for $10 per year. New Schools Exchange, 2840 Hidden Valley Lane, Santa Barbara, California 93103.

TEACHER DROP-OUT CENTER

The Teacher Drop-Out Center seeks to discover schools at all levels, public and private, that want the unusual teacher: the one who wants to make education relevant; the one who truly believes in letting students grow into individual, alive and aware humans; the one who breathes controversy and innovation. It also seeks to find these same unusual teachers, teachers who are finding it difficult to function freely as individuals with their own sense of style, teachers who see the classroom as a place for controversial ideas and innovations, teachers who want to be more than babysitters. The Center functions as a clearing house (free of charge) matching teachers and schools to their mutual advantage. Write: Teacher Drop-Out Center, Box 521, Amherst, Massachusetts 01002.

WORLD FUTURE SOCIETY

The Society's objectives are 1) to contribute to a reasoned awareness of the future and of the importance of its study, without advocating particular ideologies or engaging in political activities; 2) to advance responsible and serious investigation of the future; 3) to promote the development and improvement of methodologies for the study of the future; 4) to increase public understanding of future-oriented activities and studies; and 5) to facilitate communication and cooperation among organizations and individuals interested in studying or planning for the future. In addition to its publication, *The Futurist,* the Society publishes a supplementary *Bulletin* giving information concerning publications, meetings, research projects, bibliography, etc. The Society maintains a Document Depository, a Speakers Bureau and a Book Service for its members. Membership in the

Society, including a subscription to *The Futurist*, is $7.50. World Future Society, P.O. Box 19285, Twentieth Street Station, Washington, D.C. 20036.

ECOLOGY ACTION

Ecology Action provides services to educate, inform and otherwise assist interested persons in organizing to deal with the growing ecological problems of our culture. EA assists fledgling groups and individuals with printed information concerning ecological realities and attitudes, sets up exhibits and organizes community workshops in attempts to involve the general public in the quest for sound ecological solutions. EA has prepared a text and teacher aid for public school use entitled *What's Ecology?* Ecology Action Educational Institute, Box 9334, Berkeley, California 94709.

THIS MAGAZINE IS ABOUT SCHOOLS

This Magazine is About Schools is, as critics and the editors agree, a "mixed bag of diverting criticism, practical visions, and handy guerrilla tactics for teachers, students, and parents." The scope of its concerns is revealed in articles ranging from the natural harmonies of work and play among American Indians to prospects for honesty in sex education, from unorthodox designs for learning environments to the experience of making a movie about a street gang. Subscriptions are $4 a year. Address: 56 Esplanade Street East, Suite 401, Toronto 215, Ontario, Canada.

LEARNING EXCHANGES

Basically, the learning exchange is a "switchboard" matching service. Individuals register name, telephone number, and area of interest with the exchange. The exchange then matches, by exchange of phone numbers, persons wanting to learn with those wanting to teach in a specific area. Learning exchanges are generally staffed by volunteers, and cost next-to-nothing to operate. Their services are free, although some teachers may wish to charge for their knowledge. Ultimately, learning exchanges have the potential to form a network of access to nearly every resource person in a community. Learning exchanges currently operate in several cities. For example: Evanston Learning Exchange, 828 Davis Street, Evanston, Illinois 60202; St. Louis Learning Resources Exchange, 4552 McPherson Avenue, St. Louis, Missouri 63122; Openings Network, 613 Winans Way, Baltimore, Maryland 21229. The Center for Curriculum Design wishes to receive addresses of additional learning exchanges, so we can share them with others.

THE TEACHER PAPER

The Teacher Paper is a magazine recording the experience of the working classroom teacher. It presents teacher problems, teacher successes, teacher failures. It contains candid anecdotes from the classroom, the playground and the faculty lounge. It publishes only teachers, though its "letters" section is open to anyone — parents, students, teachers, administrators, university people. The Teacher Paper is also an

audience, mostly teachers, but also numerous parents,
kids and administrators — all of whom know they are
not alone in their vision of what decent schools and
classrooms are all about. Subscriptions are $2 a year.
Address: 280 North Pacific Avenue, Monmouth,
Oregon 97361.

**BIG ROCK CANDY MOUNTAIN:
A LEARNING TO LEARN CATALOGUE**

Everything we learn is only real to the degree that it
contributes to what we are. Direct knowledge of
ourselves, the reality of the world we live in, and the
facilitation of our inner growth and change are the
ultimate goals of education. For the most part, self-
knowledge has been limited to mysticism, psycho-
analysis, and various beyond-the-fringe activities, and
education has been limited to a culturally determined
range of ideas and techniques. We have been es-
tranged from the knowledge of ourselves; it is no
wonder that we are left empty by the present educational process both in and out of school. The Big
Rock Candy Mountain seeks to aid in the acquisition
of this knowledge: not by molding the learner into a
pre-established pattern, but by providing resources to
help him quench his thirst; not by teaching meaningless stockpiling leading to a dissatisfied life, but by
encouraging growth in the present leading toward a
joyous old age; not by changing people, but by awak-
ening a desire to change. This is our motivation for
doing this catalogue. Subscription: $8 per year, which
includes two main catalogues and four smaller infor-

218

mal ones. Available from the Portola Institute, Inc.,
1115 Merrill Street, Menlo Park, California 94025.

SOURCE, THE ORGANIZER'S CATALOG

Source Catalog, growing out of work done by the
Education Liberation Front (ELF), is a guide toward
radical change, a resource encyclopedia of counter-
institutional services, community-controlled projects,
and organizing tools for institutional takeover. Divided into 13 major liberation areas (e.g., communications, health, justice, environment, economics, education), the complete catalog will fill 13 volumes. *Communications*, the first issue, lists over 400 books,
tapes, periodicals, films useful as communications resources; and catalogs how to get in touch with 500
radical print and media groups: film co-ops, community-controlled TV, political art and music groups,
street theater, FCC license-challenging, listener-con-
trolled radio, radical libraries, etc. *Communities*, the
second catalog issue, is planned for spring 1972. The
Source Collective (2115 S Street NW, Washington,
D.C. 20008) welcomes suggestions. Source Catalog is
available in bookstores at $1.50, or from the publish-
er, Swallow Press, 1139 South Wabash, Chicago,
Illinois 60605.

THE SUMMERHILL SOCIETY

The Summerhill Society is a national organization of
persons actively concerned with truly democratic education, holding to the premise that when children
are given a responsible freedom in a climate of under-

standing and non-possessive love, they choose with wisdom, learn with alacrity, and develop genuine social attitudes. The Society publishes a bulletin six times a year, as a means for members and schools to keep in touch. Their October 1969, issue is a valuable bibliography of books and articles on the free school movement, and is available for fifty cents. The Summerhill Society, 339 Lafayette Street, New York, New York 10012.

CIDOC

The Centro Intercultural de Documentation, a center for higher learning co-founded by Ivan Illich for the de-Yankeefication of Latin American studies, is becoming a principal center for profound analysis and criticism of the inherent inadequacy of schools to provide mass education. Numerous Center seminars and a growing body of the Center's literature are devoted to a consideration of alternatives to schooling. Persons with a particular interest in deeply penetrating socioeconomic perspectives on alternative futures for education should write Everett Reimer at CIDOC, Rancho Tetela, Apdo. 479, Cuernevaca, Morelos, Mexico.

THE COUNCIL ON ECONOMIC PRIORITIES

CEP is an independent center for research and information on the social implications of corporation policies and practices. Individuals and institutions interested in selective buying, selective investing, consumer boycotts, and proxy fights in terms of the "social conscience" of various corporations find solid data in CEP studies. CEP focuses on four social issues: 1) preservation of a wholesome environment, 2) fair employment practices, 3) production of war materials, and 4) overseas investments. Publications include a journal *(Economic Priorities Report)* and in-depth studies (e.g., on pollution and the paper-pulp industry). Some studies are adapted for commercial paperbacks: *Efficiency in Death: The Manufacturers of Anti-Personnel Weapons* (Harper & Row); for students, *A Guide to Corporations: Where They Stand*, a summary of 45 companies that recruit on campuses (1972 Holt, Rinehart & Winston). Membership in CEP and subscription to their publications are offered in different categories; special rates for students and clergy. Address: 1028 Connecticut Avenue, N.W., Washington, D.C. 20036.

CALIFORNIA INSTITUTE OF THE ARTS

The California Institute of the Arts is a school for counter-education in which everyone is both student and teacher; where there is collaboration among highly creative people engaged in theater, film, design, music, and painting. The challenge of establishing a total art environment has stimulated the most innovative kinds of artistic, literary, and educational processes. The lesson is that traditional educational patterns have grown so stifling that the mere act of planning a new art school, free university, commune, or even a single course, which abandons the paraphernalia of conventional schooling, will itself release significant energies. Many seem to agree that more genuine learning occurred while revolts were in progress in such widely separated settings as the Sorbonne, Columbia, Berkeley, and Hornsey, than at earlier or later points. The problem at the California Institute of the Arts in particular, and the problem of counter-education in general, would seem to be that of establishing an educational environment in which radical energy can be sustained, deepened, and transformed before and after confrontation. California Institute of the Arts knows of no better advice than was provided by the Sorbonne counter-educator who coined the graffiti, "Je suis marxiste, tendance Groucho." The dean of California Institute of the Arts would only add, however, that some Americans seem to do their best work when they follow Harpo. California Institute of the Arts, 2404 West 7th, Los Angeles, California.

THE MOTHER EARTH NEWS

If you are more interested in living than *making* a living, if you would rather live *with* the earth than on it, if the organic life is more appealing to you than the mechanical one, *The Mother Earth News* is your kind of magazine. Sixty-plus pages per issue, with heavy emphasis on alternative life styles, ecology, working with nature, and doing more with less. Single copy $1.00. Subscriptions: $5.00 per year (6 issues), $9.00 for two years. *The Mother Earth News,* P.O. Box 38, Madison, Ohio 44507.

POPULATION INSTITUTE

The Institute, whose first major activity was the sponsorship of the Spring 1970 Gathering on Human Ecology at Buck Hill Falls, Pennsylvania, promotes and provides information about institutional and *ad hoc* population and environmental study. The Institute publishes a brief but highly informational free newsletter, *Popins,* and provides models and consultation services for the organization of regional and statewide action-oriented meetings of faculty-student teams who desire to advance population/environmental study and education. Population Institute, 100 Maryland Avenue, N.E., Washington, D.C. 20002.

FIRST FOUNDATION JOURNAL

"This journal is a strange beast indeed. Pessimism and hope. On one hand it discusses matter-of-factly the impending doom of society and what each of us can do to protect ourselves, and on the other it pretends that nothing of the sort is going to happen." Inspired by the work of Isaac Asimov in his "Foundation trilogy," it aims to chronicle the possibilities of man's survival. Subscriptions for four issues are $7 per year. Foundation, P.O. Box 14096, Minneapolis, Minnesota 55414.

Information on additional programs and materials is available in a packet from the Center for Curriculum Design, 823 Foster Street, Evanston, Illinois 60204. The cost of this packet, including Can Man Care for the Earth?, *is $5.*